FIGHTERS 1914–1919

ATTACK AND TRAINING AIRCRAFT

The Pocket Encyclopedia
of World Aircraft in Color

FIGHTERS 1914–1919
ATTACK AND TRAINING AIRCRAFT

by
KENNETH MUNSON

Illustrated by
JOHN W. WOOD
Michael Baber
Norman Dinnage
William Hobson
Alan Holliday
Tony Mitchell
Allen Randall

MACMILLAN PUBLISHING CO., INC.
NEW YORK

Macmillan Publishing Co., Inc.
866 Third Avenue, New York, N.Y. 10022

Library of Congress Catalog Card Number 68–20155

First American Edition 1969
Second American Edition 1976

Color printed by The Ysel Press, Deventer, Holland
Text printed and books bound in England
by Richard Clay (The Chaucer Press), Ltd.,
Bungay, Suffolk

PREFACE

So far as the colour plates in this volume are concerned, we owe an incalculable debt of gratitude to Ian D. Huntley, A.M.R.Ae.S., whose extensive researches have provided the basis for all of the colour work in this volume. A short account of Ian Huntley's researches – and a few of the results that they have yielded – appear in the Appendices. These, if read in conjunction with the notes on page 16, should obviate a number of misconceptions which apparently confused some readers of the first edition.

For help or reference material of other kinds, I am indebted to material published by the American journal *Air Progress*, by Harleyford Publications Ltd. and by Profile Publications Ltd. Individual assistance with the original edition, also much appreciated, was given by Messrs. Charles F. Andrews of BAC, Bo Widfelt of the Swedish Aviation Historical Society, and Lt. Col. N. Kindberg of the Royal Swedish Air Force; this revised edition has benefited in no small measure from material kindly made available subsequently by Chaz Bowyer, Jack Bruce, Roland Eichenberger, Peter L. Gray and Douglas Pardee. To them all I am delighted to express again my thanks, both for their kindness and for the helpful spirit in which their assistance was offered.

May 1975

INTRODUCTION

When war broke out in Europe in August 1914, aircraft designed to fight one another in the air did not exist. Indeed, the people whose business it was to acquire aeroplanes for the armies and navies of most of the warring nations seemed almost unanimous in thinking that aeroplanes had little, if any, practical application for war purposes. It was grudgingly conceded that they might be of some use, as an adjunct to the existing military and naval forces, to observe the progress of the war; but as regards their making any positive contribution to that progress, such a possibility received scant support or encouragement. France, which was as far-sighted as any of the committed countries where aviation was concerned, did have aeroplanes in service capable of bombing the enemy; but even there, in the home of European aviation, many of those in official positions felt that the aeroplane was little more than 'a substitute for the captive balloon'.

As early as 1911, Major Brooke-Popham of the Air Battalion, Royal Engineers, fitted a gun on to his Blériot monoplane – and was very quickly ordered by his superiors to take it off again. Colonel Isaac Newton Lewis, who demonstrated the possibilities of fitting one of his machine-guns on a Wright biplane of the United States Army Signal Corps, was met with such little enthusiasm that he left the country in disgust and in 1913 set up a factory at Liège in Belgium to manufacture his guns there.

It was the war itself, therefore, that created the need for the fighter. The first R.F.C. machines sent across to France were flown by crews instructed to use their aircraft to ram any Zeppelins encountered on the way: it was the only means they had of bringing down the enemy. Since parachutes and life jackets were then unknown, the prospect of such an encounter was scarcely calculated to raise the morale of pilots with no previous experience of combat. They made the best of it and wrapped themselves in old motor-car tyres as a precaution against having to come down in the Channel on their way to the Front.

During the first few months, aircraft of both sides were sent over enemy lines to report the progress of troop movements or the accuracy of their own artillery fire against enemy positions. Before long they found themselves under attack from 2-seaters whose observers had begun to carry pistols or rifles into the air with them. They, in their turn, having also been built without a given armament, could only retaliate in like fashion, and in this sporadic way the foundations of aerial fighting came into being.

Most of these early aeroplanes, it must be admitted, were scarcely of the kind that could have indulged in much aerial fighting even if they had been equipped with better armament. They were frail and slow, and they would have been slowed down even more if they had had to carry the weight of a machine-gun and ammunition as well. Only a handful of 'high-speed scouts', as they were known, were available – aircraft like the Sopwith Tabloid and Bristol Scout. They had top speeds around 90 m.p.h. (145 km/hr.) and the structural strength and ability to manoeuvre that would have made them useful fighting machines if they had had anything effective to fight with. But, like their slower compatriots, the best that they could hope for was the hand-held gun or one on a rudimentary mounting alongside the fuselage or above the wing. Of the weapons available, the one-shot cavalry carbine was the one most commonly favoured, but service revolvers and duck rifles were among the wide and often bizarre assortment of weapons carried.

At this distance in time, and in an age of sophisticated aeroplane armament, it is a matter for some wonder that with such elementary weapons any crew was ever successful in shooting down an opponent. It was virtually impossible for the pilot of a single-seat aircraft to fly his machine and manage a hand-held weapon of any kind, and therefore it was usually the 2-seaters that were armed in this fashion, the gun being fired by the observer. Considering that at this period of the war the standard arrangement of most 2-seaters was to seat the observer in the front cockpit, where he had the engine cylinders in front of him, struts and wires on either side and the pilot behind him, he usually had little worthwhile field of fire at all, and the risk of a bullet fracturing a bracing wire – or, more important, a control wire – was not inconsiderable. Yet, despite the difficulties, several successes were achieved with hand-held guns operated under these conditions.

It was, of course, the machine-gun that transformed the aero-plane into a real fighting machine, and it did so to deadly purpose in 1915. The Lewis and the little French Hotchkiss were the first machine-guns to go regularly into the air, followed by one or another variant of the pre-war Maxim infantry machine-gun. This was built in Germany at the Spandau arsenal, the pre-war LMG.08 being generally known as the Parabellum and its 1915 modification, the LMG.08/15, being known to the Allies simply as the Spandau. The British-built Vickers machine-gun was also a Maxim variant.* Throughout the major part of the war the Parabellum was the standard German observer's gun and the Lewis the Allied equivalent. The Spandau and Vickers were the most commonly used pilots' guns.

When Germany introduced its C type observation aircraft in the spring of 1915 the observer was transferred to the rear seat, a more logical position that gave him a much less obstructed outlook and the freedom to fire his gun in many more directions. These aircraft were, however, still vulnerable to an attacker that could approach them with forward-firing guns, but so far the only machines regularly carrying such guns were the pusher-engined types whose propellers, being at the rear, did not interfere with the forward firing of the gun. The inherently clumsy layout of a pusher machine meant, however, that it was usually less fast, and often less manoeuvrable, than the German observation machines which were mostly tractor types. Clearly, therefore, the next move was to combine the performance of a tractor aeroplane with the ability to employ a front-mounted gun. One solution was the mounting of the gun over the top wing and elevating it to fire upward at about 45 degrees so that the bullets passed outside the area swept by the revolving propeller blades. This method proved quite successful, and indeed was retained on a number of fighter types in service much later in the war, especially those engaged in combating the Zeppelin menace. However, the more significant approach was that which led eventually to a means of firing the gun between the propeller blades as they revolved in such a way that none of the bullets would strike and damage the propeller.

Before the outbreak of war, Franz Schneider of L.V.G. and Ray-

* The names Parabellum, Spandau and Vickers have been used throughout this volume for the sake of clarity.

mond Saulnier of Morane-Saulnier had each worked, in Germany and France respectively, on ways of achieving this by relating the rate of fire of a machine-gun to the rate of revolution of a propeller. Schneider patented a primitive mechanical gear of this kind in July 1913, and a revised form of it was installed on the L.V.G. E.VI monoplane in 1915, the first German aircraft to be fitted with such a device. This machine was destroyed while on its way to the Front to be tested operationally, and no further examples of it were built. The French authorities were unwilling to back continued research by Raymond Saulnier into the same problem, despite some encouraging early results. Roland Garros suggested the next best thing: if the firing of the gun could not be interrupted as the propeller blades passed in front of it, then the occasional bullet would have to be allowed to strike the blades and a means would have to be devised of protecting the blades themselves from damage. This was done by fitting small wedge-shaped deflector plates made of steel to each blade to divert the passage of those bullets that struck them. This device was first introduced into combat by Garros, a pupil of Santos-Dumont and a pre-war exhibition pilot, who had the propeller of his Morane-Saulnier L parasol monoplane fitted with these deflector plates and took it back to his squadron in March 1915. Up until that time no pilot over the Western Front had had any reason to fear being fired upon by a tractor-type aeroplane coming straight towards him. Garros was quick to exploit the surprise value of his unique machine, but his success was short-lived. On 18 April 1915 he was obliged to make a forced landing inside enemy lines. He and his aircraft were captured before he could destroy it completely, and an attempt was quickly made to reproduce the deflection device for use on German aircraft. This proved unsuccessful – it is said because the plates were not strong enough to withstand the steel-jacketed German bullets. Anthony Fokker was then asked to make a fresh attempt to copy the French device, but instead he decided to go one better. Fokker is generally credited personally with the successful evolution of the first fully-practical gun interrupter gear, but it is now virtually certain* that the actual design of the gear was the work of Heber, Leimberger and Luebbe, three of his engineering

* See *Profile No. 38: The Fokker Monoplanes*, by J. M. Bruce, M.A. (Profile Publications Ltd., 1965.)

staff at Schwerin. The Fokker M.5K monoplane, on which the efficacy of the new interrupter mechanism was first successfully demonstrated, received the military designation E.I and was the first of the Fokker monoplane fighters.

Having developed an offensive weapon, the German air service did not immediately exploit it for offensive purposes, for the Fokker E types were at first assigned for local defence and protective escort work with squadrons flying observation 2-seaters. Not until the late autumn of 1915, when it was fully realised that the Allies had no effective counter-weapon, did the Fokker 'scourge' really begin in earnest, and throughout the 1915–16 winter they virtually commanded the skies over western Europe. They acquired a reputation far in excess of their technical merit, notwithstanding their superior firepower, for they were not especially fast and were not employed in tremendous numbers. Their main victim was the poorly-armed, ultra-stable (and therefore almost unmanoeuvrable) B.E.2c, which was too restricted in performance to have much chance either of evading them or of hitting back. The Fokkers' success came because they were virtually unopposed, and it is a more realistic measure of their real combat worth that two of the three types mainly responsible for ending their supremacy were pusher types, the D.H.2 and the F.E.2b.

The D.H.2 and its fellow Fokker-beaters brought the margin of superiority in the air back to the Allies until the first Albatros and Halberstadt tractor biplane fighters appeared later in 1916, and from then until the end of the war the pendulum of air supremacy swung first one way and then the other as each side in turn developed counter-weapons to the other's latest fighters. The third member of the Allied trio, the little Nieuport 11, in many respects typified fighter aircraft of the remaining period of the war and beyond. It was small, light, agile and had a reliable rotary engine, and it favoured an overwing gun firing outside the propeller arc. As the pattern of fighter aircraft development began to take shape, two separate lines of thought began to emerge. The first and more successful placed the main emphasis on flying qualities and agility in the air, while the other placed a higher premium on additional engine and gun power, even at the price of performance. It was proved repeatedly that a nimble, single-gun fighter could fly rings round a heavier two-gun machine, and it was not until the final year or so of the war that two-gun fighters appeared in quantity with a manoeuvrability to compare with the best of the single-gun fighters of 1916–17. By the end of the war, however, the two-gun fighter was the accepted standard, and speeds of around 120 m.p.h. (193 km/hr.) were by no means exceptional.

The stimulus given to aeroplane development by the evolution of better fighters had its effect upon other categories of aircraft, and led to the first signs of specialisation of roles such as shipboard fighters, ground attack and armoured close support machines. It brought to the fore the talents of some of the design geniuses whose names were to become bywords – de Havilland, Heinkel, Junkers and others.

Common targets for fighter aircraft were the Zeppelin airships employed extensively by Germany and Austro-Hungary and the observation balloons used widely by both sides. They could not always be shot down satisfactorily by the normal machine-gun armament, even when incendiary bullets were used, and other means were devised for attacking them. Often airships were destroyed by dropping steel-tipped darts or small high-explosive bombs from an aircraft flying over them. The machine-gun (or, less often, the Allied Le Prieur electrically-fired rocket) were the most usual weapons employed for 'balloon-busting', an occupation that demanded an aircraft with a good low-level performance. Harassment of ground forces from the air was a popular occupation of the German CL types, among others. These were originally brought into being as protective escorts for the larger C type observation machines, but once they were fitted with a forward-firing gun in addition to the observer's rear gun they became very effective at ground attack work.

To keep the picture in a proper perspective, it is necessary to appreciate the conditions under which aircraft and crews had to carry out their combat duties. Most fighter-to-fighter engagements, especially during the latter half of the war, were carried out at heights between 10,000 and 20,000 feet (approx. 3,000 to 6,000 metres) with the crews in open cockpits, with no oxygen breathing equipment and wearing unheated flying suits. The intense cold at these heights affected not only the physical efficiency of the fliers but the lubrication and cooling systems of their engines and guns. Gun stoppages were still an all-too-frequent occurrence, even in excellent late-war fighters like the Fokker D.VII and S.E.5a, and often an engagement had to be broken off when something like this happened. (Once gun synchronisation became a standard practice, designers often thought to improve the aerodynamic performance of their machines by installing the guns within the engine cowling or in some other location where they would create less drag to reduce the aeroplane's speed. They quickly learned, however, that it was better to sacrifice a few miles per hour off the top speed for the sake of having the guns immediately in front of the cockpit where the pilot could get to them to clear them when a stoppage occurred.) While on the ground, the aircraft were either pegged down in the open or, at best, stored in field hangars made only of canvas, and the depredations to their fabric caused by the bitter cold of the Russian Front, the miserable dampness of the Western Front or the blistering Middle Eastern heat can be imagined. The performance figures recorded for individual types are those obtaining under more or less ideal flying conditions; but it should be remembered that for much of the time such conditions were not enjoyed.

The rapid expansion of the air forces of all the major combatants as the war progressed had a profound effect on each country industrially as well as strategically. Only in Austria, France, Germany and the U.S.A. were there aircraft industries worthy of the name when the war started; in Britain, Italy and Russia they were to all intents and purposes created by the war. This expansion produced a need for organised flying training on an unprecedented scale, and although by far the greater part of such training was given on obsolete combat types 'retired' from front-line service there were a select few types which made their names chiefly on account of their contribution to the training programme, notably the Avro 504 and the Curtiss JN-4, the wartime output of which was comparable to that of some of the leading combat machines.

THE COLOUR PLATES

As an aid to identification, the eighty colour plates which follow have been arranged on a visual basis, within the broad sequence: pusher biplanes, tractor biplanes, tractor triplanes, tractor monoplanes, flying boats and seaplanes. The 'split' plan view is adopted to give upper and lower surface markings within a single plan outline. The reference number of each aircraft corresponds to the appropriate text matter, and an index to all types appears on pages 187 to 188.

To clarify some apparent misconceptions arising from the first edition:

(a) It should not be assumed, from the 'split' plan view presentation, that the unseen portion of the plan view of a camouflaged aircraft is a 'mirror image' of the half that is portrayed;

(b) It should not be assumed that all colour plates are intended to show standard colour schemes or a pristine 'ex-works' state of finish. Indeed, several plates deliberately show 'weathered' aircraft;

(c) Note (b) above applies particularly to the British khaki/ P.C.10 colouring (see Appendix 2) which, within the limitations of the colour reproduction process, an attempt has been made to illustrate in a wide variety of conditions, from an ex-works aircraft with maximum 'green shift' (e.g. page 69) to a much weathered aircraft (e.g. page 75).

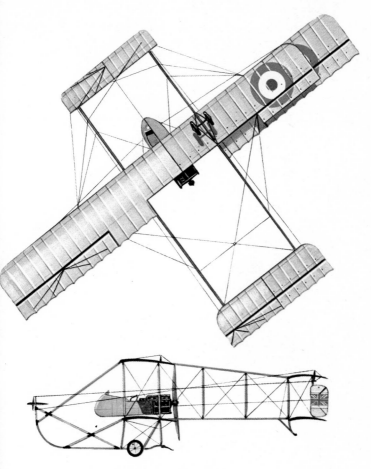

1

Maurice Farman MF.7 (S.7) of an R.N.A.S. training unit, *ca.* early 1915.
Engine: One 70 h.p. Renault air-cooled Vee-type. *Span:* 51 ft. 0 in. (15·54
m.). *Length:* 37 ft. $2\frac{7}{8}$ in. (11·35 m.). *Wing area:* 645·8 sq. ft. (60·00 sq.
m.). *Take-off weight:* 1,885 lb. (855 kg.). *Maximum speed:* 59 m.p.h. (95
km./hr.) at sea level. *Service ceiling:* approx. 13,123 ft. (4,000 m.). *Endurance:*
approx. 3 hr. 30 min.

D.H.1A (U.K.)

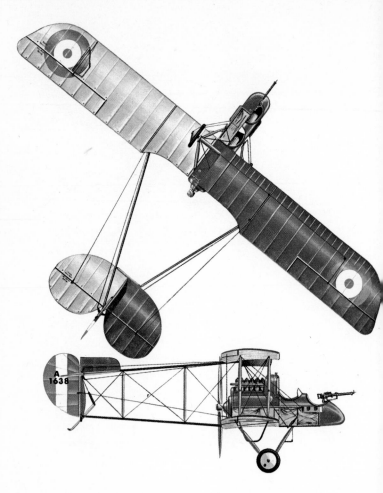

2

Savages-built D.H.1A of No. 14 Squadron R.F.C., Palestine, *ca.* April 1917. *Engine:* One 120 h.p. Beardmore water-cooled in-line. *Span:* 41 ft. 0 in. ee·50 m.). *Length:* 28 ft. 11¼ in. (8·82 m.). *Wing area:* 362·25 sq. ft. (33·47 sq. m.). *Take-off weight:* 2,340 lb. (1,061 kg.). *Maximum speed:* 88 m.p.h. (141·6 km./hr.) at 4,000 ft. (1,219 m.). *Service ceiling:* 13,500 ft. (4,115 m.). *Endurance:* approx. 2 hr. 30 min.

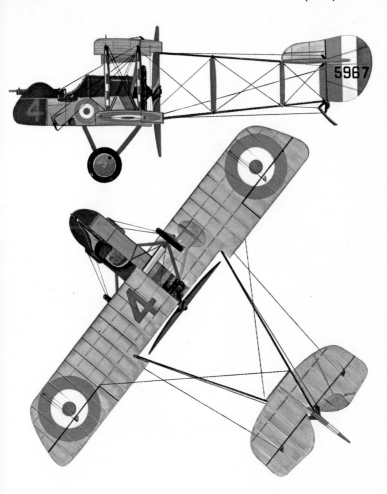

3

Airco-built D.H.2 of 'A' Flight, No. 24 Squadron R.F.C., Bertangles, spring 1916. *Engine:* One 100 h.p. Gnome Monosoupape rotary. *Span:* 28 ft. 3 in. (8·61 m.). *Length:* 25 ft. 2½ in. (7·68 m.). *Wing area:* 249·0 sq. ft. (23·13 sq. m.). *Take-off weight:* 1,441 lb. (654 kg.). *Maximum speed:* 93 m.p.h. (149·7 km./hr.) at sea level. *Service ceiling:* 14,500 ft. (4,420 m.). *Endurance:* 2 hr. 45 min.

F.E.2b (U.K.)

4

Boulton & Paul-built F.E.2b, possibly an aircraft of No. 20 Squadron R.F.C., France, *ca.* spring 1916. *Engine:* One 120 h.p. Beardmore water-cooled in-line. *Span:* 47 ft. 9 in. (14·55 m.). *Length:* 32 ft. 3 in. (9·83 m.). *Wing area:* 494·0 sq. ft. (45·89 sq. m.). *Take-off weight:* 2,967 lb. (1,346 kg.). *Maximum speed:* 80·5 m.p.h. (129·6 km./hr.) at sea level. *Service ceiling:* 9,000 ft. (2,743 m.). *Endurance:* 2 hr. 30 min.

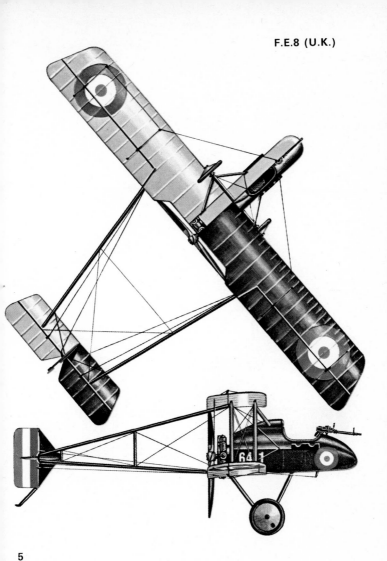

F.E.8 (U.K.)

5

Darracq-built F.E.8 of No. 40 or 41 Squadron R.F.C., France, late 1916.
Engine: One 100 h.p. Gnome Monosoupape rotary. *Span:* 31 ft. 6 in. (9·60 m.). *Length:* 23 ft. 8 in. (7·21 m.). *Wing area:* 218·0 sq. ft. (20·25 sq. m.). *Take-off weight:* 1,346 lb. (611 kg.). *Maximum speed:* 94 m.p.h. (151·3 km./hr.) at sea level. *Service ceiling:* 14,500 ft. (4,420 m.). *Endurance:* approx. 4 hr. 0 min.

VICKERS F.B.5 (U.K.)

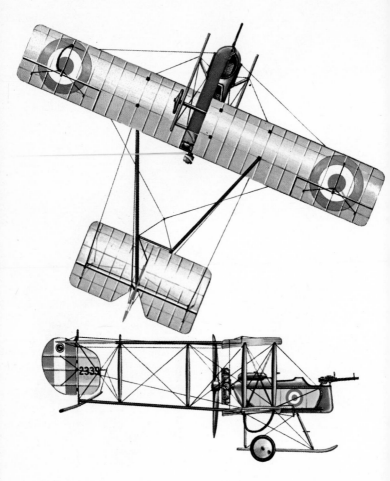

6

Vickers-built F.B.5 'Gunbus', possibly an aircraft of No. 11 Squadron R.F.C., *ca*. spring 1915. *Engine:* One 100 h.p. Gnome Monosoupape rotary. *Span:* 36 ft. 6 in. (11·13 m.). *Length:* 27 ft. 2 in. (8·28 m.). *Wing area:* 382·0 sq. ft. (35·49 sq. m.). *Take-off weight:* 2,050 lb. (930 kg.). *Maximum speed:* 70 m.p.h. (112·6 km./hr.) at 5,000 ft. (1,524 m.). *Service ceiling:* 9,000 ft. (2,743 m.). *Endurance:* 4 hr. 0 min.

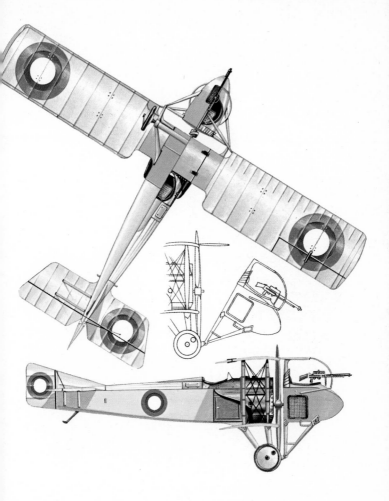

7

Spad A2 of the Imperial Russian Air Service, 1915. *Engine:* One 80 h.p. Le Rhône rotary. *Span:* 31 ft. 4 in. (9·55 m.). *Length:* 23 ft. 11 in. (7.29 m.). *Wing area:* 272·3 sq. ft. (25·30 sq. m.). *Take-off weight:* 1,797 lb. (815 kg.). *Maximum speed:* 69·6 m.p.h. (112 km./hr.) at sea level. *Service ceiling:* 9,843 ft. (3,000 m.). *Endurance:* 2 hr. 0 min.

HANNOVER CL.IIIa (Germany)

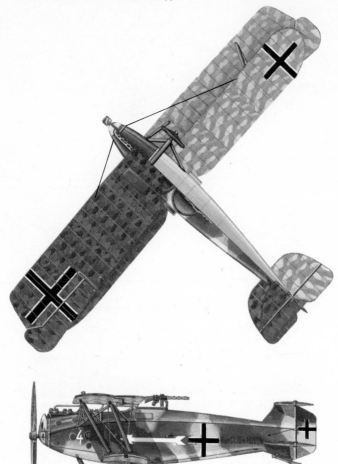

8

Hannover CL.IIIa of the Imperial German Military Aviation Service, shot down 2 October 1918 by Capt. E. V. Rickenbacker and Lt. Reed Chambers of the 94th Aero Squadron, A.E.F. *Engine:* One 180 h.p. Argus As.III water-cooled in-line. *Span:* 38 ft. 4⅔ in. (11·70 m.). *Length:* 24 ft. 10⅜ in. (7·58 m.). *Wing area:* 352·0 sq. ft. (32·70 sq. m.). *Take-off weight:* 2,381 lb. (1,080 kg.). *Maximum speed:* 102·5 m.p.h. (165 km./hr.) at 1,968 ft. (600 m.). *Service ceiling:* 24,606 ft. (7,500 m.). *Endurance:* 3 hr. 0 min.

HALBERSTADT CL.II (Germany)

9

Halberstadt CL.II of the Imperial German Military Aviation Service, *ca.* May 1918. *Engine:* One 160 h.p. Mercedes D.III water-cooled in-line. *Span:* 35 ft. 4 in. (10·77 m.). *Length:* 23 ft. 11⅜ in. (7·30 m.). *Wing area:* 296·0 sq. ft. (27·50 sq. m.). *Take-off weight:* 2,498 lb. (1,133 kg.). *Maximum speed:* 102·5 m.p.h. (165 km./hr.) at 16,400 ft. (5,000 m.). *Service ceiling:* 16,732 ft. (5,100 m.). *Endurance:* 3 hr. 0 min.

LUSAC-11 (U.S.A.)

10

Packard-Le Père LUSAC-11 of the U.S. Army Air Service, late 1918. *Engine:* One 425 h.p. Liberty 12 water-cooled Vee-type. *Span:* 41 ft. 7 in. (12·67 m.). *Length:* 25 ft. 3 in. (7·70 m.). *Wing area:* 415·6 sq. ft. (38·61 sq. m.). *Take-off weight:* 3,746 lb. (1,699 kg.). *Maximum speed:* 136 m.p.h. (218·9 km./hr.) at sea level. *Service ceiling:* 20,200 ft. (6,157 m.). *Range:* 320 miles (515 km.).

BRISTOL FIGHTER (U.K.)

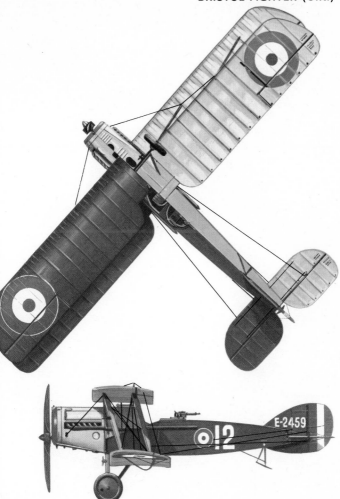

11

Bristol-built F.2B of 'B' Flight, No. 88 Squadron R.A.F., France, summer 1918. *Engine:* One 275 h.p. Rolls-Royce Falcon III water-cooled Vee-type. *Span:* 39 ft. 3 in. (11·96 m.). *Length:* 25 ft. 10 in. (7·87 m.). *Wing area:* 405·6 sq. ft. (37·68 sq. m.). *Take-off weight:* 2,848 lb. (1,292 kg.). *Maximum speed:* 123 m.p.h. (198 km./hr.) at 5,000 ft. (1,524 m.). *Service ceiling:* 18,000 ft. (5,486 m.). *Endurance:* 3 hr. 0 min.

CURTISS JN-3 (U.S.A.)

12

Curtiss JN-3 of an R.N.A.S. training unit, autumn 1916 (rebuilt by The Fairey Aviation Co. Ltd., incorporating rudder and other components from JN-4A). *Engine:* One 90 h.p. Curtiss OX-5 water-cooled Vee-type. *Span:* 43 ft. 7⅜ in. (13·29 m.). *Length:* 27 ft. 4 in. (8·33 m.). *Wing area:* 352·0 sq. ft. (32·70 sq. m.). *Take-off weight:* 2,130 lb. (966 kg.). *Maximum speed:* 75 m.p.h. (120·7 km./hr.) at sea level. *Service ceiling:* 11,000 ft. (3,353 m.). *Endurance:* 2 hr. 15 min. (Weight and performance are for similar JN-4D.).

13

Grahame-White-built D.H.6 of an R.F.C. training unit in the U.K., early 1917. *Engine:* One 90 h.p. R.A.F. 1a air-cooled Vee-type. *Span:* 35 ft. $11\frac{1}{8}$ in. (10·95 m.). *Length:* 27 ft. $3\frac{1}{2}$ in. (8·32 m.). *Wing area:* 436·3 sq. ft. (40·53 sq. m.). *Take-off weight:* 2,027 lb. (919 kg.). *Maximum speed:* 66 m.p.h. (106·2 km./hr.) at 6,500 ft. (1,981 m.). *Service ceiling:* 10,000 ft. (3,048 m.). *Range:* approx. 195 miles (314 km.).

B.E.12 (U.K.)

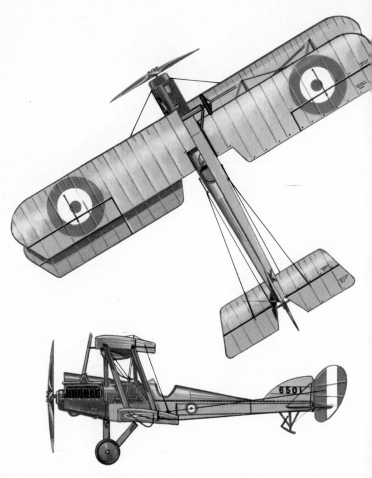

14

Daimler-built B.E.12 of the R.F.C., France, autumn 1916. *Engine:* One 150 h.p. R.A.F.4a air-cooled Vee-type. *Span:* 37 ft. 0 in. (11·28 m.). *Length:* 27 ft. 3 in. (8·31 m.). *Wing area:* 371·0 sq. ft. (34·47 sq. m.). *Take-off weight:* 2,352 lb. (1,067 kg.). *Maximum speed:* 102 m.p.h. (164·2 km./hr.) at sea level. *Service ceiling:* 12,500 ft. (3,810 m.). *Endurance:* 3 hr. 0 min.

PHÖNIX D.III (Austro-Hungary)

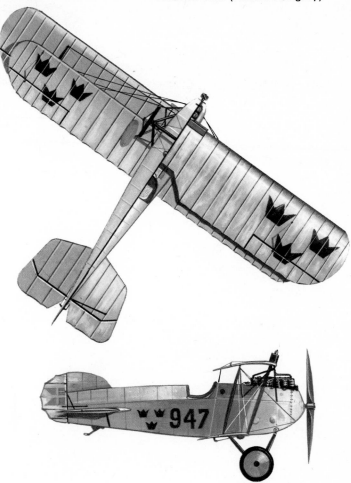

15

Phönix-built D.III of the Royal Swedish Army Aviation, *ca.* summer 1919; now displayed in the R.Sw.A.F. Museum, Malmslatt. *Engine:* One 230 h.p. Hiero water-cooled in-line. *Span:* 32 ft. 1⅞ in. (9·80 m.). *Length:* 21 ft. 8⅝ in. (6·62 m.). *Wing area:* 269·1 sq. ft. (25·00 sq. m.). *Take-off weight:* 2,097 lb. (951 kg.). *Maximum speed:* 121·2 m.p.h. (195 km./hr.) at sea level. *Service ceiling:* 22,310 ft. (6,800 m.). *Endurance:* 2 hr. 0 min.

HANSA-BRANDENBURG D.I (Austro-Hungary)

16

Phönix-built D.I Series 28 of the Austro-Hungarian Air Service, late 1916. *Engine:* One 160 h.p. Austro-Daimler water-cooled in-line. *Span:* 27 ft. 10½ in. (8·50 m.). *Length:* 20 ft. 10 in. (6·35 m.). *Wing area:* 257·8 sq. ft. (23·95 sq. m.). *Take-off weight:* 2,028 lb. (920 kg.). *Maximum speed:* 118·1 m.p.h. (190 km./hr.) at sea level. *Service ceiling:* 16,404 ft. (5,000 m.). *Endurance:* approx. 2 hr. 30 min.

AVIATIK D.I (Austro-Hungary)

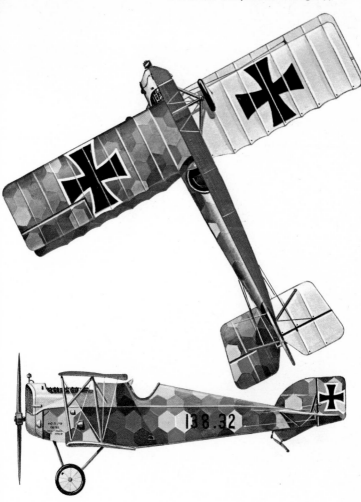

17

Austrian Aviatik (Berg) D.I of the Austro-Hungarian Air Service, late 1917. *Engine:* One 200 h.p. Austro-Daimler water-cooled in-line. *Span:* 26 ft. 3 in. (8·00 m.). *Length:* 22 ft. 9⅜ in. (6·95 m.). *Wing area:* 234·7 sq. ft. (21·80 sq. m.). *Take-off weight:* 1,878 lb. (852 kg.). *Maximum speed:* 115 m.p.h. (185 km./hr.) at sea level. *Service ceiling:* 20,177 ft. (6,150 m.). *Endurance:* 2 hr. 30 min.

HALBERSTADT D.II (Germany)

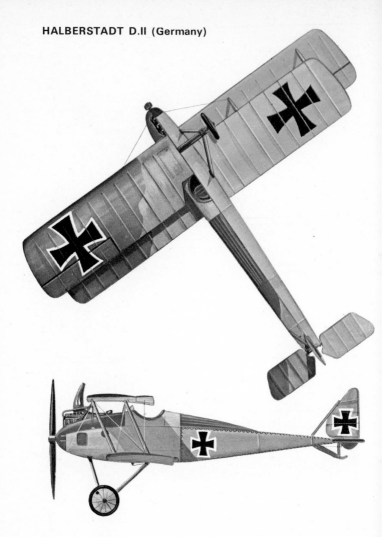

18

Halberstadt D.II of the Imperial German Military Aviation Service, *ca.* autumn 1916. *Engine:* One 120 h.p. Mercedes D.II water-cooled in-line. *Span:* 28 ft. 10½ in. (8·80 m.). *Length:* 23 ft. 11⅜ in. (7·30 m.). *Wing area:* approx. 244·9 sq. ft. (22·75 sq. m.). *Take-off weight:* 1,609 lb. (730 kg.). *Maximum speed:* 90·1 m.p.h. (145 km./hr.) at sea level. *Service ceiling:* approx. 13,000 ft. (4,000 m.). *Endurance:* approx. 1 hr. 30 min.

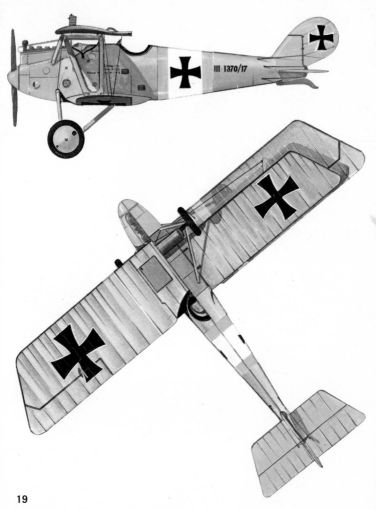

19

Pfalz D.III flown by Vizefeldwebel Hecht of *Jasta* 10, Imperial German Military Aviation Service, September 1917. *Engine:* One 160 h.p. Mercedes D.III water-cooled in-line. *Span:* 30 ft. $10\frac{1}{8}$ in. (9·40 m.). *Length:* 22 ft. $9\frac{2}{3}$ in. (6·95 m.). *Wing area:* 238·6 sq. ft. (22·17 sq. m.). *Take-off weight:* 2,055 lb. (932 kg.). *Maximum speed:* 102·5 m.p.h. (165 km./hr.) at 9,843 ft. (3,000 m.). *Service ceiling:* 17,060 ft. (5,200 m.). *Endurance:* 2 hr. 30 min.

ROLAND D.II (Germany)

20

L.F.G. (Roland) D.II of the Imperial German Military Aviation Service, *ca.* spring 1917. *Engine:* One 160 h.p. Mercedes D.III water-cooled in-line. *Span:* 29 ft. 4 in. (8·94 m.). *Length:* 22 ft. 8⅞ in. (6·93 m.). *Wing area:* 245·4 sq. ft. (22·80 sq. m.). *Take-off weight:* 1,753 lb. (795 kg.). *Maximum speed:* 105 m.p.h. (169 km./hr.) at sea level. *Service ceiling:* approx. 16,404 ft. (5,000 m.). *Endurance:* 2 hr. 0 min.

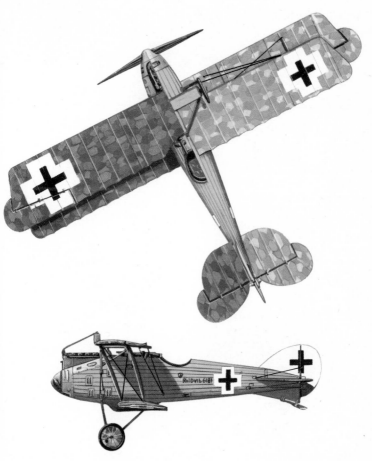

21

L.F.G. (Roland) D.VIb for the Imperial German Military Aviation Service, June 1918. *Engine:* One 150/200 h.p. Benz Bz.IIIa water-cooled in-line. *Span:* 30 ft. 10⅛ in. (9·40 m.). *Length:* 20 ft. 8¾ in. (6·32 m.). *Wing area:* 238·2 sq. ft. (22·13 sq. m.). *Take-off weight:* 1,896 lb. (860 kg.). *Maximum speed:* 113·4 m.p.h. (182·5 km./hr.) at 6,562 ft. (2,000 m.). *Service ceiling:* 19,030 ft. (5,800 m.). *Endurance:* 2 hr. 0 min.

ALBATROS D.II (Germany)

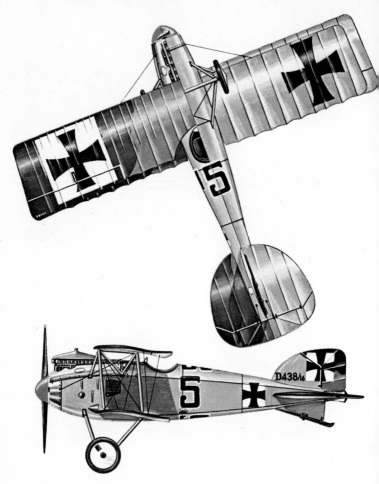

22

Albatros D.II of the Imperial German Military Aviation Service, *ca.* November 1916. *Engine:* One 160 h.p. Mercedes D.III water-cooled in-line. *Span:* 27 ft. 10⅔ in. (8·50 m.). *Length:* 24 ft. 3⅓ in. (7·40 m.). *Wing area:* 263·7 sq. ft. (24·50 sq. m.). *Take-off weight:* 1,958 lb. (888 kg.). *Maximum speed:* 108·7 m.p.h. (175 km./hr.) at sea level. *Service ceiling:* 17,060 ft. (5,200 m.). *Endurance:* 1 hr. 30 min.

ALBATROS D.III (Germany)

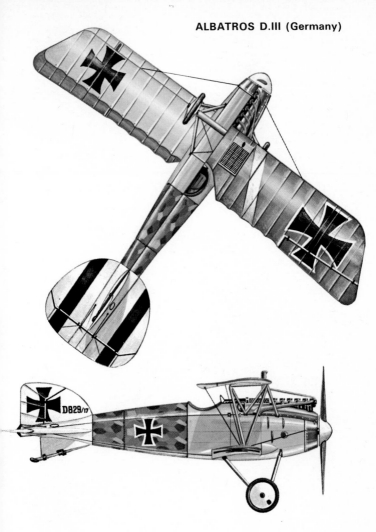

23

Albatros D.III of the Imperial German Military Aviation Service which crashed north of Savoy in October 1917. *Engine:* One 160/175 h.p. Mercedes D.IIIa water-cooled in-line. *Span:* 29 ft. 8⅓ in. (9·05 m.). *Length:* 24 ft. 0⅝ in. (7·33 m.).*Wing area:* 220·7 sq. ft. (20·50 sq. m.). *Take-off weight:* 1,953 lb. (886 kg.).*Maximum speed:* 108·7 m.p.h. (175 km./hr.) at 3,280 ft. (1,000 m.). *Service ceiling:* 18,045 ft. (5,500 m.). *Endurance:* 2 hr. 0 min.

ALBATROS D.Va (Germany)

24

Albatros D.Va of *Jasta* 5, Imperial German Military Aviation Service, early 1918. *Engine:* One 170/185 h.p. Mercedes D.IIIa water-cooled in-line. *Span:* 29 ft. 8⅓ in. (9·05 m.). *Length:* 24 ft. 0⅝ in. (7·33 m.). *Wing area:* 228·2 sq. ft. (21·20 sq. m.). *Take-off weight:* 2,066 lb. (937 kg.). *Maximum speed:* 116 m.p.h. (187 km./hr.) at 3,280 ft. (1,000 m.). *Service ceiling:* 20,505 ft. (6,250 m.). *Endurance:* 2 hr. 0 min.

S.E.5a (U.K.)

25

Royal Aircraft Factory-built S.E.5a flown by Capt. K. L. Caldwell, commanding No. 74 Squadron R.F.C., France, March 1918. *Engine:* One 200 h.p. Wolseley W.4a Viper water-cooled Vee-type. *Span:* 26 ft. 7⅜ in. (8·11 m.). *Length:* 20 ft. 11 in. (6·38 m.). *Wing area:* 245·8 sq. ft. (22·84 sq. m.). *Take-off weight:* 1,988 lb. (902 kg.). *Maximum speed:* 120 m.p.h. (193·1 km./hr.) at 15,000 ft. (4,572 m.). *Service ceiling:* 19,500 ft. (5,944 m.). *Endurance:* 3 hr. 0 min.

PFALZ D.XII (Germany)

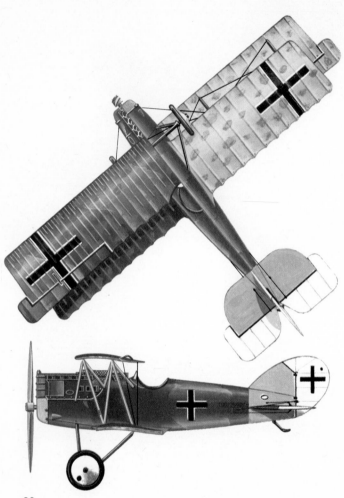

26

Pfalz D.XII (*Jasta* unidentified) of the Imperial German Military Aviation Service, captured by the French in October 1918. *Engine:* One 180 h.p. Mercedes D.IIIa water-cooled in-line. *Span:* 29 ft. 6⅓ in. (9·00 m.). *Length:* 20 ft. 10 in. (6·35 m.). *Wing area:* 233·6 sq. ft. (21·70 sq. m.). *Take-off weight:* 1,978 lb. (897 kg.). *Maximum speed:* 105·6 m.p.h. (170 km./hr.) at 9,843 ft. (3,000 m.). *Service ceiling:* 18,536 ft. (5,650 m.). *Endurance:* 2 hr. 30 min.

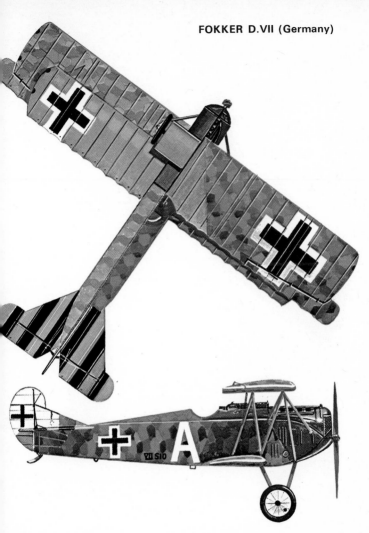

FOKKER D.VII (Germany)

27

D.VII (possibly Albatros-built), believed to be an aircraft of *Jasta* 17, Imperial German Military Aviation Service, *ca.* May 1918. *Engine:* One 160 h.p. Mercedes D.III water-cooled in-line. *Span:* 29 ft. 2⅓ in. (8·90 m.). *Length:* 22 ft. 9¾ in. (6·95 m.). *Wing area:* 220·7 sq. ft. (20·50 sq. m.). *Take-off weight:* 1,984 lb. (900 kg.). *Maximum speed:* 117·4 m.p.h. (189 km./hr.) at 3,280 ft. (1,000 m.). *Service ceiling:* 19,685 ft. (6,000 m.). *Endurance:* 1 hr. 30 min.

ELEPHANT (U.K.)

28

Martinsyde G.102 'Elephant' of No. 27 Squadron R.F.C., Western Front, late 1916/early 1917. *Engine:* One 120 h.p. Beardmore water-cooled in-line. *Span:* 38 ft. 0 in. (11·58 m.). *Length:* 26 ft. 6½ in. (8·09 m.). *Wing area:* 410·0 sq. ft. (38·09 sq. m.). *Take-off weight:* 2,424 lb. (1,099 kg.). *Maximum speed:* 95 m.p.h. (152·9 km./hr.) at 6,500 ft. (1,981 m.). *Service ceiling:* 14,000 ft. 4,267 m.). *Endurance:* 5 hr. 30 min.

29

Martinsyde F.4 Buzzard Mk. I in R.A.F. markings, used at RAE Farnborough 1919. *Engine:* One 300 h.p. Hispano-Suiza 8 Fb water-cooled Vee-type. *Span:* 32 ft. 9⅜ in. (9·99 m.). *Length:* 25 ft. 5⅝ in. (7·76 m.). *Wing area:* 320·0 sq. ft. (29·73 sq. m.). *Take-off weight:* 2,398 lb. (1,088 kg.). *Maximum speed:* 132·5 m.p.h. (213 km./hr.) at 15,000 ft. (4,572 m.). *Service ceiling:* 24,000 ft. (7,315 m.).

SPAD VII (France)

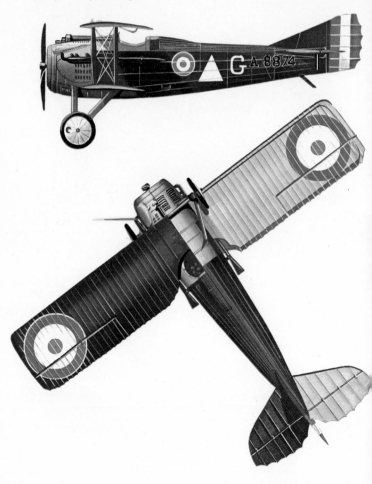

30

British Blériot & Spad Co.-built Spad VII of No. 23 Squadron R.F.C., La Lovie, autumn 1917. *Engine:* One 150 h.p. Hispano-Suiza 8 Aa water-cooled Vee-type. *Span:* 25 ft. 7¾ in. (7·82 m.). *Length:* 20 ft. 2⅛ in. (6·15 m.). *Wing area:* 193·8 sq. ft. (18·00 sq. m.). *Take-off weight:* 1,632 lb. (740 kg.). *Maximum speed:* 119 m.p.h. (191·5 km./hr.) at 6,562 ft. (2,000 m.). *Service ceiling:* 17,500 ft. (5,334 m.). *Endurance:* 2 hr. 15 min.

SPAD XIII (France)

31

Spad XIIIC.1 of the 213th Aero Squadron A.E.F., Western Front, summer 1918. *Engine:* One 235 h.p. Hispano-Suiza 8 Be water-cooled Vee-type. *Span:* 26 ft. 4⅞ in. (8·08 m.). *Length:* 20 ft. 4⅞ in. (6·22 m.). *Wing area:* 227·7 sq. ft. (21·15 sq. m.). *Take-off weight:* 1,808 lb. (820 kg.). *Maximum speed:* 133·6 m.p.h. (215 km./hr.) at 6,562 ft. (2,000 m.). *Service ceiling:* 21,818 ft. (6,650 m.). *Endurance:* 2 hr. 0 min.

AUSTIN-BALL A.F.B.1 (U.K.)

32

First prototype A.F.B.1, early 1917. *Engine:* One 200 h.p. Hispano-Suiza water-cooled Vee-type. *Span:* 30 ft. 0 in. (9·14 m.). *Length:* 21 ft. 6 in. (6·55 m.). *Wing area:* 290·0 sq. ft. (26·94 sq. m.). *Take-off weight:* 2,077 lb. (942 kg.). *Maximum speed:* 138 m.p.h. (222 km./hr.) at sea level. *Service ceiling:* 22,000 ft. (6,706 m.). *Endurance:* 2 hr. 15 min.

33

Sopwith-built 5F.1 Dolphin Mk. I of 'B' Flight, No. 79 Squadron R.F.C., Champien, February 1918. *Engine:* One 200/220 h.p. Hispano-Suiza 8 E water-cooled Vee-type. *Span:* 32 ft. 6 in. (9·91 m.). *Length:* 22 ft. 3 in. (6·78 m.). *Wing area:* 263·25 sq. ft. (24·46 sq. m.). *Take-off weight:* 2,003 lb. (908 kg.). *Maximum speed:* 128 m.p.h. (206 km./hr.) at 10,000 ft. (3,048 m.). *Service ceiling:* 21,000 ft. (6,400 m.). *Endurance:* 1 hr. 45 min.

ANSALDO A.1 (Italy)

34

Ansaldo A.1 *Balilla* of the *Corpo Aeronautica Militare, ca.* summer 1918.
Engine: One 220 h.p. SPA 6A water-cooled in-line. *Span:* 25 ft. 2⅓ in. (7·68 m.). *Length:* 22 ft. 5¼ in. (6·84 m.). *Wing area:* 228·2 sq. ft. (21·20 sq. m.). *Take-off weight:* 1,951 lb. (885 kg.). *Maximum speed:* 136·7 m.p.h. (220 km./hr.) at 6,562 ft. (2,000 m.). *Service ceiling:* 16,404 ft. (5,000 m.). *Endurance:* 1 hr. 30 min.

35

Nieuport-Delage 29C.1 flown by Lt. Casale of the French *Aviation Militaire* to a world altitude record of 9,520 m. (32,233·6 ft.) on 14 June 1919; now displayed in the *Musée de l'Air*, Paris. *Engine:* One 300 h.p. Hispano-Suiza 8 Fb water-cooled Vee-type. *Span:* 32 ft. 0 in. (9·75 m.). *Length:* 21 ft. 5⅞ in. (6·55 m.). *Wing area:* 288·5 sq. ft. (26·80 sq. m.). *Take-off weight:* 2,535 lb. (1,150 kg.). *Maximum speed:* 142·9 m.p.h. (230 km./hr.) at sea level. *Service ceiling:* 27,231 ft. (8 300 m.). *Range:* 373 miles (600 km.).

BANTAM (U.K.)

36

B.A.T. F.K.23 Bantam Mk. I, fifth production aircraft in R.A.F. colours, autumn 1918. *Engine:* One 170 h.p. A.B.C. Wasp I air-cooled radial. *Span:* 25 ft. 0 in. (7·62 m.). *Length:* 18 ft. 5 in. (5·61 m.). *Wing area:* 185·0 sq. ft. (17·19 sq. m.). *Take-off weight:* 1,321 lb. (599 kg.). *Maximum speed:* 128 m.p.h. (206 km./hr.) at 6,500 ft. (1,981 m.). *Service ceiling:* 20,000 ft. (6,096 m.). *Endurance:* 2 hr. 15 min.

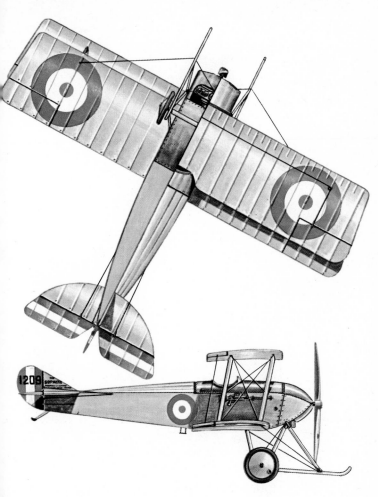

37

Sopwith-built Tabloid of the R.N.A.S., late 1914. *Engine:* One 80 h.p. Gnome rotary. *Span:* 25 ft. 6 in. (7·77 m.). *Length:* 20 ft. 4 in. (6·20 m.). *Wing area:* 241·3 sq. ft. (22·42 sq. m.). *Take-off weight:* 1,120 lb. (508 kg.). *Maximum speed:* 92 m.p.h. (148 km./hr.) at sea level. *Service ceiling:* approx. 15,000 ft. (4,572 m.). *Endurance:* 3 hr. 30 min.

S.E.2 (U.K.)

38

S.E.2 at the Royal Aircraft Factory, Farnborough, early 1914. *Engine:* One 80 h.p. Gnome rotary. *Span:* 27 ft. 6¼ in. (8·39 m.). *Length:* 20 ft. 6 in. (6·25 m.). *Wing area:* approx. 190·0 sq. ft. (17·65 sq. m.). *Take-off weight:* 1,200 lb. (544 kg.). *Maximum speed:* 96 m.p.h. (154·5 km./hr.) at sea level. *Service ceiling:* approx. 15,000 ft. (4,572 m.). *Endurance:* approx. 2 hr. 30 min.

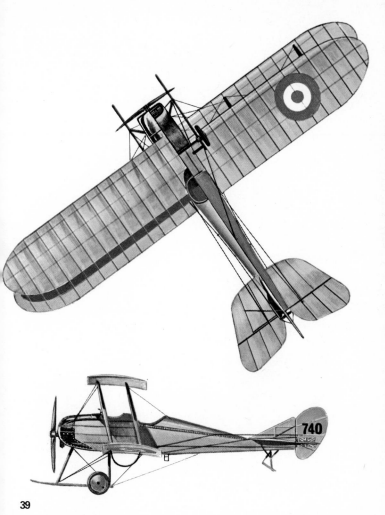

39

B.E.8 (probably Vickers-built) of No. 8 Squadron R.F.C., France, June 1915.
Engine: One 80 h.p. Gnome rotary. *Span:* 39 ft. 6 in. (12·04 m.). *Length:*
27 ft. 3 in. (8·31 m.). *Wing area:* approx. 420·0 sq. ft. (39·02 sq. m.). *Take-off
weight:* approx. 1,850 lb. (839 kg.). *Maximum speed:* 70 m.p.h. (112·6 km./hr.)
at sea level. *Service ceiling:* approx. 10,000 ft. (3,048 m.). *Endurance:* approx.
2 hr. 30 min.

AVRO 504J (U.K.)

40

Avro-built 504J of 'A' Flight, No. 1 School of Special Flying R.F.C., Gosport, November 1917. *Engine:* One 100 h.p. Gnome Monosoupape rotary. *Span:* 36 ft. 0 in. (10·97 m.). *Length:* 29 ft. 5 in. (8·97 m.). *Wing area:* 330·0 sq. ft. (30·66 sq. m.). *Take-off weight:* 1,800 lb. (816 kg.). *Maximum speed:* 82 m.p.h. (131·9 km./hr.) at 6,500 ft. (1,981 m.). *Service ceiling:* 13,000 ft. (3,962 m.). *Endurance:* 3 hr. 0 min.

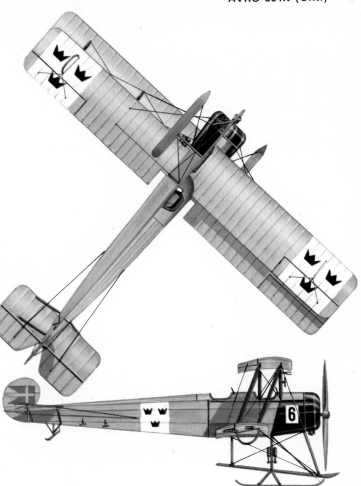

41

Avro 504K of the Royal Swedish Naval Aviation, *ca.* 1920. *Engine:* One 130 h.p. Clerget 9 B rotary. *Span:* 36 ft. 0 in. (10·97 m.). *Length:* 29 ft. 5 in. (8·97 m.). *Wing area:* 330·0 sq. ft. (30·66 sq. m.). *Take-off weight:* 1,830 lb. (830 kg.). *Maximum speed:* approx. 105 m.p.h. (168·9 km./hr.) at 6,500 ft. (1,981 m.). *Service ceiling:* 19,000 ft. (5,791 m.). *Endurance:* approx. 2 hr. 45 min.

BRISTOL SCOUT (U.K.)

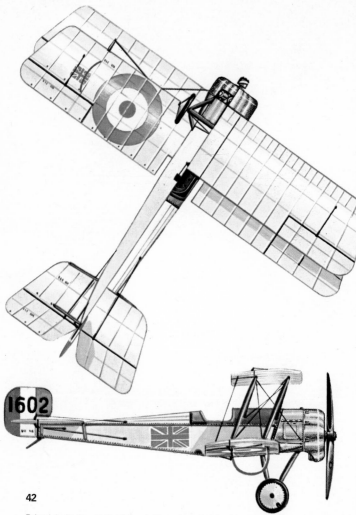

42

Bristol-built Scout C of No. 1 Squadron R.F.C., France, May 1915. *Engine:* One 80 h.p. Gnome rotary. *Span:* 24 ft. 7 in. (7·49 m.). *Length:* 20 ft. 8 in. (6·30 m.). *Wing area:* 198·0 sq. ft. (18·39 sq. m.). *Take-off weight:* 1,200 lb. (544 kg.). *Maximum speed:* 92·7 m.p.h. (149·2 km./hr.) at sea level. *Service ceiling:* 15,500 ft. (4,724 m.). *Endurance:* 2 hr. 30 min.

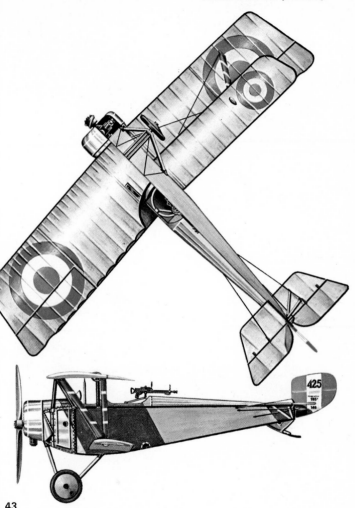

43

Nieuport 12C.2 of the French *Aviation Militaire, ca.* autumn 1915. *Engine:* One 130 h.p. Clerget 9 B rotary. *Span:* 29 ft. 7½ in. (9·03 m.). *Length:* 23 ft. 11⅞ in. (7·30 m.). *Wing area:* 236·8 sq. ft. (22·00 sq. m.). *Take-off weight:* 2,028 lb. (920 kg.). *Maximum speed:* 96·2 m.p.h. (155 km./hr.) at sea level. *Service ceiling:* 15,420 ft. (4,700 m.). *Endurance:* approx. 2 hr. 45 min.

NIEUPORT 11 (France)

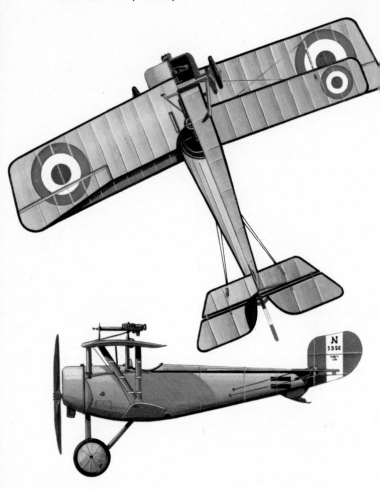

44

Nieuport 11C.1 of the French *Aviation Militaire, ca.* spring 1916. *Engine:* One 80 h.p. Le Rhône 9 C rotary. *Span:* 24 ft. 9¼ in. (7·55 m.). *Length:* 19 ft. 0½ in. (5·80 m.). *Wing area:* 139·9 sq. ft. (13·00 sq. m.). *Take-off weight:* 1,058 lb. (480 kg.). *Maximum speed:* 96·8 m.p.h. (156 km./hr.) at sea level. *Service ceiling:* 15,092 ft. (4,600 m.). *Endurance:* 2 hr. 30 min.

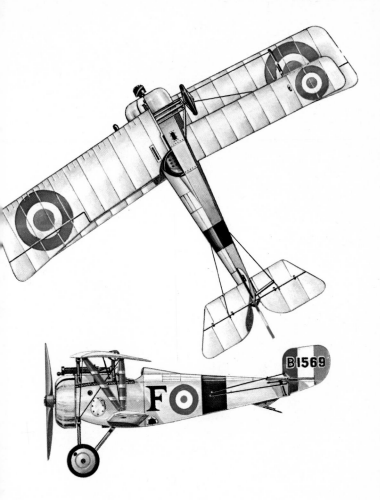

45

Nieuport 17C.1, believed to be an aircraft of No. 1 Squadron R.F.C., France, *ca.* April 1917. *Engine:* One 110 h.p. Le Rhône 9 J rotary. *Span:* 26 ft. 11⅝ in. (8·22 m.).. *Length:* 18 ft. 10 in. (5·74 m.). *Wing area:* 158·8 sq. ft. (14·75 sq. m.). *Take-off weight:* 1,246 lb. (565 kg.). *Maximum speed:* 110 m.p.h. (177 km./hr.) at 6,562 ft. (2,000 m.). *Service ceiling:* 17,388 ft. (5,300 m.). *Endurance:* 2 hr. 0 min.

NIEUPORT 27 (France)

46

Nieuport 27C.1 of the French *Aviation Militaire*, 1917. *Engine:* One 120 h.p. Le Rhône 9 Jb rotary. *Span:* 26 ft. 10$\frac{7}{8}$ in. (8·20 m.). *Length:* 19 ft. 2$\frac{1}{3}$ in. (5·85 m.). *Wing area:* 161·5 sq. ft. (15·00 sq. m.). *Take-off weight:* 1,289 lb. (5855 kg.). *Maximum speed:* 115·6 m.p.h. (186 km./hr.) at sea level. *Service ceiling:* 18,208 ft. (5,550 m.). *Endurance:* approx. 1 hr. 30 min.

NIEUPORT 28 (France)

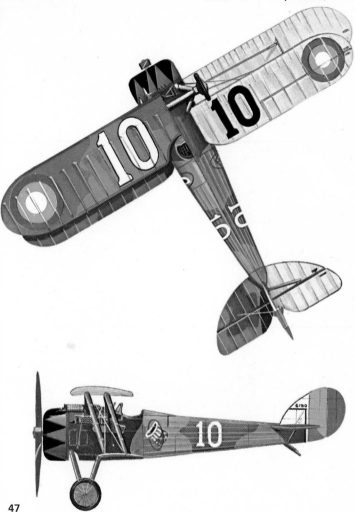

47

Nieuport 28C.1 flown by Lt. Douglas Campbell of the 94th Aero Squadron A.E.F., France, April 1918. *Engine:* One 160/170 h.p. Gnome Monosoupape 9 N rotary. *Span:* 26 ft. 8⅞ in. (8·15 m.). *Length:* 21 ft. 0 in. (6·40 m.). *Wing area:* 172·2 sq. ft. (16·00 sq. m.). *Take-off weight:* 1,625 lb. (737 kg.). *Maximum speed:* 122 m.p.h. (196·3 km./hr.) at sea level. *Service ceiling:* 17,000 ft. (5,182 m.). *Endurance:* 1 hr. 30 min.

FOKKER D.II (Germany)

48

Fokker D.II of the Imperial German Military Aviation Service, 1916. *Engine:* One 100 h.p. Oberursel U.I rotary. *Span:* 28 ft. 8½ in. (8·75 m.). *Length:* 21 ft. 0 in. (6·40 m.). *Wing area:* 193·8 sq. ft. (18·00 sq. m.). *Take-off weight:* 1,268 lb. (575 kg.). *Maximum speed:* 93·2 m.p.h. (150 km./hr.) at sea level. *Service ceiling:* 13,123 ft. (4,000 m.). *Endurance:* 1 hr. 30 min.

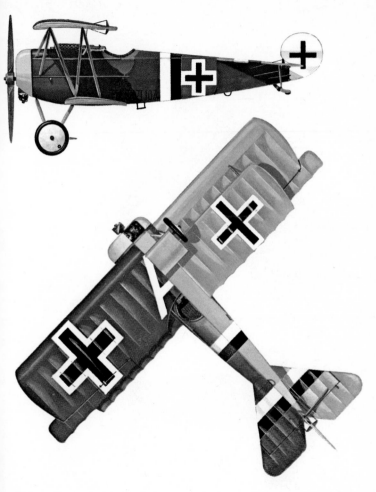

49

Fokker D.VI of the Imperial German Military Aviation Service, Russian Front, 1918. *Engine:* One 110 h.p. Oberursel UR.II rotary. *Span:* 25 ft. 1¼ in. (7·65 m.). *Length:* 20 ft. 5¼ in. (6·23 m.). *Wing area:* 190·5 sq. ft. (17·70 sq. m.). *Take-off weight:* 1,285 lb. (583 kg.). *Maximum speed:* 121·8 m.p.h. (196 km./hr.) at sea level. *Service ceiling:* 19,685 ft. (6,000 m.). *Endurance:* 1 hr. 30 min.

HANRIOT HD-1 (France)

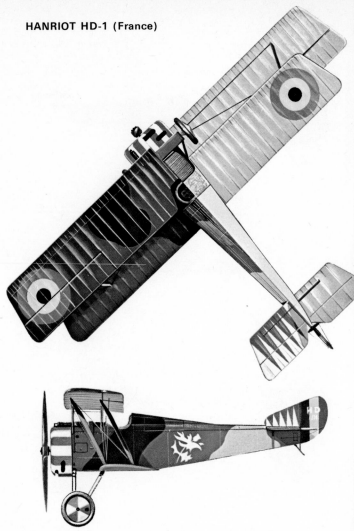

50

Hanriot HD.1 of the 1e *Escadrille*, Belgian *Aviation Militaire*, Les Moëres, 1917. *Engine:* One 120 h.p. Le Rhône 9 Jb. rotary. *Span:* 28 ft. 6½ in. (8·70 m.). *Length:* 19 ft. 2⅓ in. (5·85 m.). *Wing area:* 195·9 sq. ft. (18·20 sq. m.) *Take-off weight:* 1,334 lb. (605 kg.). *Maximum speed:* 114·3 m.p.h. (184 km./hr.) at sea level. *Service ceiling:* 19,685 ft. (6,000 m.). *Endurance:* 2 hr. 30 min.

PUP (U.K.)

51

Whitehead-built Pup used for night fighter camouflage trials at Orfordness, March 1918. *Engine:* One 80 h.p. Le Rhône 9 C rotary. *Span:* 26 ft. 6 in. (8·08 m.). *Length:* 19 ft. 3¾ in. (5·89 m.). *Wing area:* 254·0 sq. ft. (23·60 sq. m.). *Take-off weight:* 1,225 lb. (556 kg.). *Maximum speed:* 111·5 m.p.h. (179·4 km./hr.) at sea level. *Service ceiling:* 17,000 ft. (5,182 m.). *Endurance:* 3 hr. 0 min.

D.H.5 (U.K.)

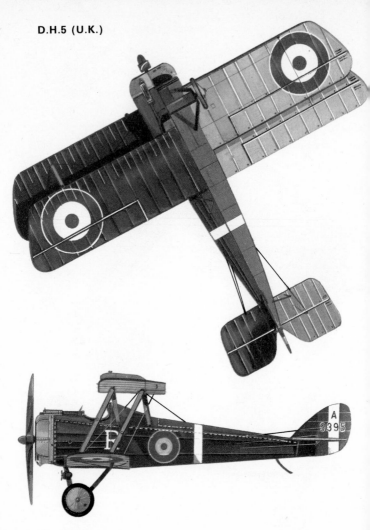

52

Darracq-built D.H.5 of No. 32 Squadron R.F.C., France, August 1917. *Engine:* One 110 h.p. Le Rhône 9 J rotary. *Span:* 25 ft. 8 in. (7·82 m.). *Length:* 22 ft. 0 in. (6·71 m.). *Wing area:* 212·1 sq. ft. (19·70 sq. m.). *Take-off weight:* 1,492 lb. (677 kg.). *Maximum speed:* 102 m.p.h. (164·2 km./hr.) at 10,000 ft. (3,048 m.). *Service ceiling:* 16,000 ft. (4,877 m.). *Endurance:* 2 hr. 45 min.

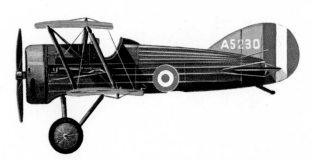

53

Vickers-built F.B.19 Mk. II of an R.F.C. Home Defence Squadron, *ca.* spring 1917. *Engine:* One 110 h.p. Le Rhône 9 J rotary. *Span:* 24 ft. 0 in. (7·32 m.). *Length:* 18 ft. 2 in. (5·54 m.). *Wing area:* 215·0 sq. ft. (19·97 sq. m.). *Take-off weight:* 1,478 lb (670 kg.). *Maximum speed:* 98 m.p.h. (157·7 km./hr.) at 10,000 ft. (3,048 m.). *Service ceiling:* 15,000 ft. (4,572 m.). *Endurance:* 3 hr. 15 min.

THOMAS-MORSE S-4 (U.S.A.)

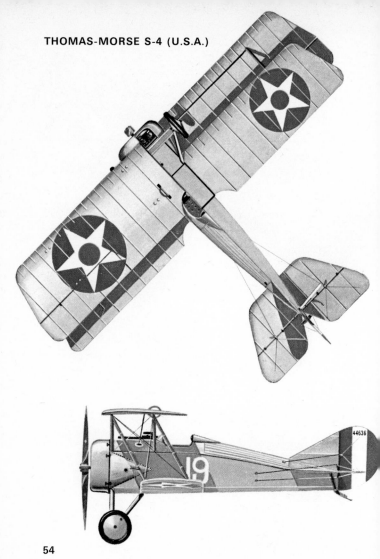

54

Thomas-Morse S-4C of the U.S. Navy, early 1918. *Engine:* One U.S.-built 80 h.p. Le Rhône 9 C rotary. *Span:* 26 ft. 6 in. (8·08 m.). *Length:* 19 ft. 10 in. (6·05 m.). *Wing area:* 234·0 sq. ft. (21·74 sq. m.). *Take-off weight:* 1,330 lb. (603 kg.). *Maximum speed:* 97 m.p.h. (156·1 km./hr.) at sea level. *Service ceiling:* 15,000 ft. (4,572 m.). *Endurance:* approx. 2 hr. 30 min.

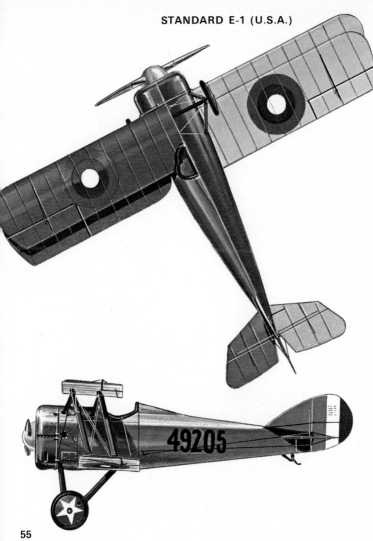

55

Standard E-1 trainer of the U.S. Army Air Service, early 1919. *Engine:* One U.S.-built 80 h.p. Le Rhône 9 C rotary. *Span:* 24 ft. 0 in. (7·32 m.). *Length:* 18 ft. 10¾ in. (5·76 m.). *Wing area:* 153·3 sq. ft. (14·24 sq m.). *Take-off weight:* 1,144 lb. (519 kg.). *Maximum speed:* 99·8 m.p.h. (160·6 km./hr.) at sea level. *Service ceiling:* 14,800 ft. (4,511 m.). *Endurance:* approx. 2 hr. 30 min.

SIEMENS-SCHUCKERT D.III (Germany)

56

Siemens-Schuckert D.III of *Jasta* 15, Imperial German Military Aviation Service, May 1918. *Engine:* One 160 h.p. Siemens-Halske Sh.III rotary. *Span:* 27 ft. 7⅞ in. (8·43 m.). *Length:* 18 ft. 8¾ in. (5·70 m.). *Wing area:* 202·6 sq. ft. (18·82 sq. m.). *Take-off weight:* 1,598 lb. (725 kg.). *Maximum speed:* 111·8 m.p.h. (180 km./hr.) at sea level. *Service ceiling:* 26,575 ft. (8,100 m.). *Endurance:* 2 hr. 0 min.

57

Boulton & Paul-built F.1 Camel of No. 65 Squadron R.A.F., France, mid-1918.
Engine: One 130 h.p. Clerget 9 B rotary. *Span:* 28 ft. 0 in. (8·53 m.). *Length:*
18 ft. 9 in. (5·72 m.). *Wing area:* 231·0 sq. ft. (21·46 sq. m.). *Take-off
weight:* 1,482 lb. (672 kg.). *Maximum speed:* 104·5 m.p.h. (168·2 km./hr.)
at 10,000 ft. (3,048 m.). *Service ceiling:* 18,000 ft. (5,486 m.). *Endurance:*
2 hr. 30 min.

SALAMANDER (U.K.)

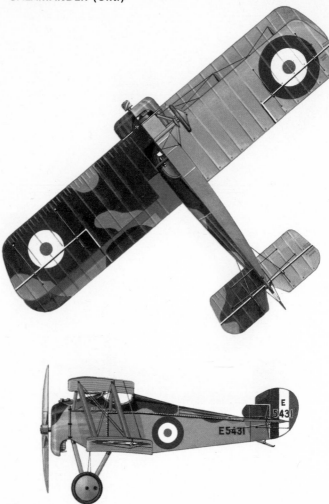

58

Sopwith-built Salamander, third prototype, illustrating a colour scheme devised for R.A.F. observation aircraft in October 1918. *Engine:* One 230 h.p. Bentley B.R.2 rotary. *Span:* 30 ft. 1½ in. (9·18 m.). *Length:* 19 ft. 6 in. (5·94 m.). *Wing area:* 266·5 sq. ft. (24·76 sq. m.). *Take-off weight:* 2,510 lb. (1,179 kg.). *Maximum speed:* 125 m.p.h. (201·1 km./hr.) at 500 ft. (152 m.). *Service ceiling:* 14,000 ft. (4,267 m.). *Endurance:* approx. 1 hr. 45 min.

59

Sopwith-built 7F.1 Snipe flown by Major W. G. Barker, V.C., while attached to No. 201 Squadron R.A.F., France, October 1918. *Engine:* One 230 h.p. Bentley B.R.2 rotary. *Span:* 30 ft. 0 in. (9·14 m.). *Length:* 19 ft. 2 in. (5·84 m.). *Wing area:* 256·0 sq. ft. (23·78 sq. m.). *Take-off weight:* 2,020 lb. (916 kg.). *Maximum speed:* 121 m.p.h. (194·7 km./hr.) at 10,000 ft. (3,048 m.). *Service ceiling:* 19,500 ft. (5,944 m.). *Endurance:* 3 hr. 0 min.

TRIPLANE (U.K.)

60

Sopwith-built triplane of No. 8 Squadron R.N.A.S., France, February 1917. *Engine:* One 130 h.p. Clerget 9 B rotary. *Span:* 26 ft. 6 in. (8·08 m.). *Length:* 19 ft. 6 in. (5·94 m.). *Wing area:* 231·0 sq. ft. (21·46 sq. m.). *Take-off weight:* 1,415 lb. (642 kg.). *Maximum speed:* 116 m.p.h. (186·7 km./hr.) at 6,000 ft. (1,823 m.). *Service ceiling:* 20,000 ft. (6,096 m.). *Endurance:* 2 hr. 45 min.

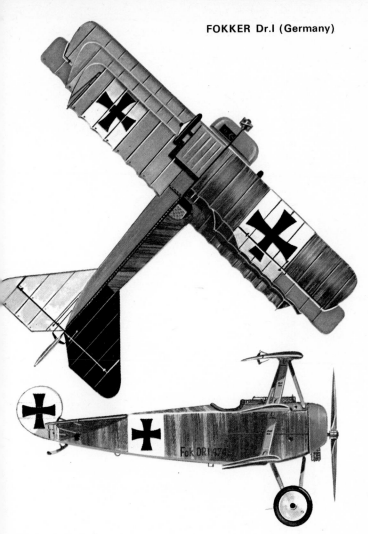

FOKKER Dr.I (Germany)

61

Fokker Dr.I, believed to be an aircraft of *Jasta* 2, Imperial German Military Aviation Service, early 1918. *Engine:* One 110 h.p. Oberursel UR.II rotary. *Span:* 23 ft. 7⅝ in. (7·19 m.). *Length:* 18 ft. 11⅛ in. (5·77 m.). *Wing area (incl. axle fairing):* 200·9 sq. ft. (18·66 sq. m.). *Take-off weight:* 1,290 lb. (585 kg.). *Maximum speed:* 102·5 m.p.h. (165 km./hr.) at 13,123 ft. (4,000 m.). *Service ceiling:* 20,013 ft. (6,100 m.). *Endurance:* 1 hr. 30 min.

MORANE-SAULNIER AI (France)

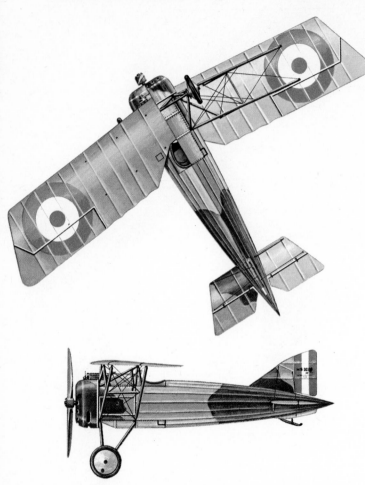

62

Morane-Saulnier MoS.29C.1 of *Escadrille* 156, French *Aviation Militaire*, January 1918. *Engine:* One 150 h.p. Gnome Monosoupape 9 N rotary. *Span:* 27 ft. 11 in. (8·51 m.). *Length:* 18 ft. 6½ in. (5·65 m.). *Wing area:* 144·1 sq. ft. (13·39 sq. m.). *Take-off weight:* 1,486 lb. (674 kg.). *Maximum speed:* 137·1 m.p.h. (220·6 km./hr.) at sea level. *Service ceiling:* 22,965 ft. (7,000 m.). *Endurance:* approx. 2 hr. 30 min.

MORANE-SAULNIER L (France)

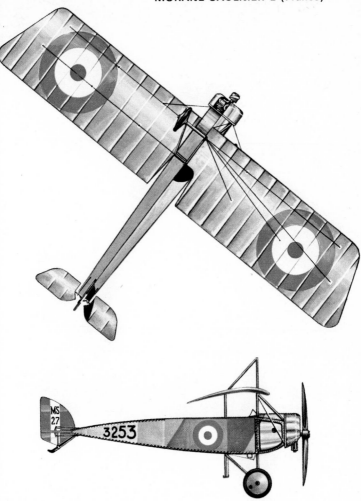

63

Morane-Saulnier MoS.3 flown by Flt. Sub-Lt. R. A. J. Warneford, V.C., of o. 1 Squadron R.N.A.S., Dunkirk, June 1915. *Engine:* One 80 hh.p. Gnome rotary. *Span:* 36 ft. 9 in. (11·20 m.). *Length:* 22 ft. 6¾ in. (6·88 m.). *Wing area:* 197·0 sq. ft. (18·30 sq. m.). *Take-off weight:* 1,499 lb. (680 kg.). *Maximum speed:* 71·5 m.p.h. (115 km./hr.) at 6,560 ft. (2,000 m.). *Service ceiling:* 13,123 ft. (4,000 m.). *Range:* 280 miles (450 km.).

FOKKER E.V (Germany)

64

Fokker E.V of *Jasta* 6, Imperial German Military Aviation Service, France, August 1918. *Engine:* One 110 h.p. Oberursel UR.II rotary. *Span:* 27 ft. 6¾ in. (8·40 m.). *Length:* 19 ft. 2¾ in. (5·86 m.). *Wing area:* 115·2 sq. ft. (10·70 sq. m.). *Take-off weight:* 1,238 lb. (562 kg.). *Maximum speed:* 115 m.p.h. (185 km./hr.) at sea level. *Service ceiling:* 20,669 ft. (6,300 m.) *Endurance:* 1 hr. 30 min.

TAUBE (Germany)

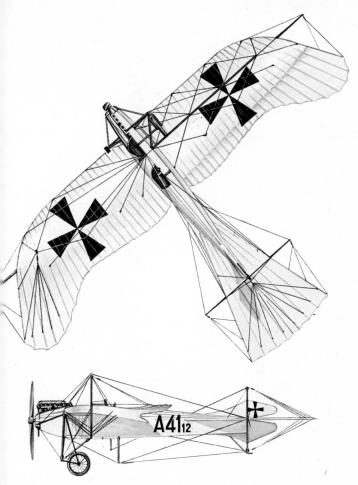

65

Taube (probably Rumpler-built) of the Imperial German Military Aviation Service, October 1914. *Engine:* One 100 h.p. Argus water-cooled in-line. *Span:* 45 ft. 11¼ in. (14·00 m.). *Length:* 33 ft. 9½ in. (10·30 m.). *Wing area:* 344·4 sq. ft. (32·00 sq. m.). *Take-off weight:* 1,190 lb. (540 kg.). *Maximum speed:* 59 m.p.h. (95 km./hr.) at sea level. *Service ceiling:* 9,843 ft. (3,000 m.). *Endurance:* 4 hr. 0 min.

MORANE-SAULNIER N (France)

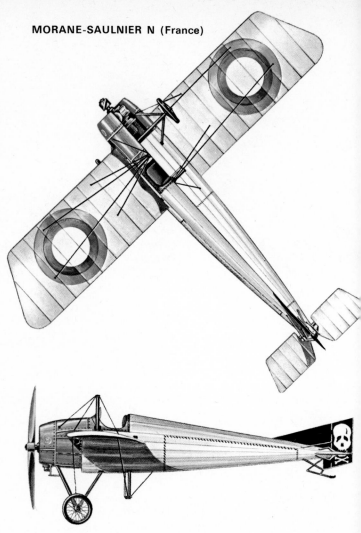

66

Morane-Saulnier MoS.6 of the XIXth Detachment, Imperial Russian Air Service, June 1915. *Engine:* One 80 h.p. Le Rhône 9 C rotary. *Span:* 26 ft. 8¾ in. (8·15 m.). *Length:* 19 ft. 1½ in. (5·83 m.). *Wing area:* 118·4 sq. ft. (11·00 sq. m.). *Take-off weight:* 979 lb. (444 kg.). *Maximum speed:* 89·5 m.p.h. (144 km./hr.). at sea level. *Service ceiling:* 13,123 ft. (4,000 m.). *Endurance:* 1 hr. 30 min.

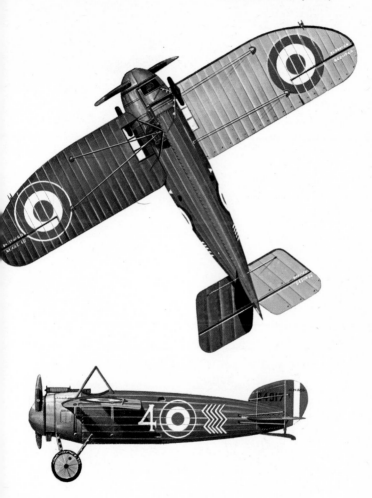

67

Bristol-built M.1C of No. 72 Squadron R.F.C., Mesopotamia, autumn 1917.
Engine: One 110 h.p. Le Rhône 9 J rotary. *Span:* 30 ft. 9 in. (9·37 m.).
Length: 20 ft. 5½ in. (6·24 m.). *Wing area:* 145·0 sq. ft. (13·47 sq. m.).
Take-off weight: 1,348 lb. (611 kg.). *Maximum speed:* 130 m.p.h. (209·2
km./hr.) at sea level. *Service ceiling:* 20,000 ft. (6,096 m.). *Endurance:* 1
hr. 45 min.

THULIN K (Sweden)

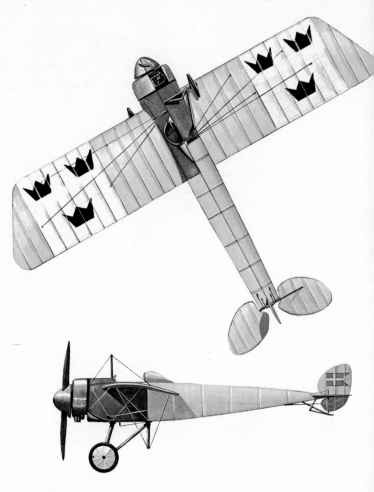

68

Thulin Type K of the Royal Swedish Army Aviation, 1917. *Engine:* One 90 h.p. Thulin Type A (improved Le Rhône 9 J) rotary. *Span:* 29 ft. 6⅓ in. (9·00 m.). *Length:* 21 ft. 7⅞ in. (6·60 m.). *Wing area:* 150·7 sq. ft. (14·00 sq. m.). *Take-off weight:* 1,157 lb. (525 kg.). *Maximum speed:* 93·2 m.p.h. (150 km./hr.) at sea level. *Service ceiling:* 18,044 ft. (5,500 m.). *Endurance:* 2 hr. 30 min.

FOKKER E.III (Germany)

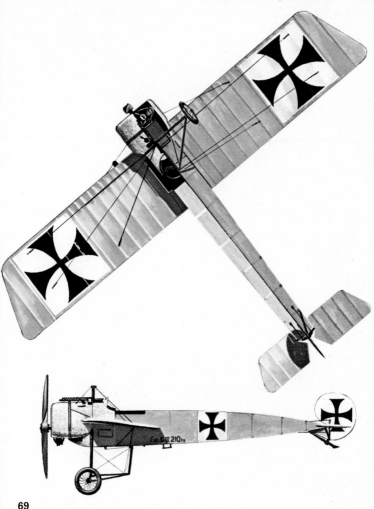

69

Fokker E.III which force-landed behind British lines in France 8 April 1916; now in possession of Science Museum, London. *Engine:* One 100 h.p. Oberursel U.I. rotary. *Span:* 31 ft. 2¾ in. (9·52 m.). *Length:* 23 ft. 11⅓ in. (7·30 m.). *Wing area:* 172·2 sq. ft. (16·00 sq. m.). *Take-off weight:* 1,400 lb. (635 kg.). *Maximum speed:* 83 m.p.h. (133·6 km./hr.) at 6,500 ft. (1,981 m.). *Service ceiling:* 11,500 ft. (3,500 m.). *Endurance:* 2 hr. 45 min.

JUNKERS D.I (Germany)

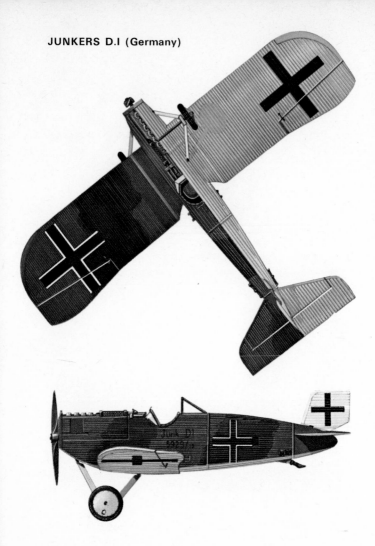

70

Junkers D.I of the Imperial German Military Aviation Service, summer 1918. *Engine:* One 160 h.p. Mercedes D.IIIaü water-cooled in-line. *Span:* 29 ft. 6¼ in. (9·00 m.). *Length:* 23 ft. 9¾ in. (7·25 m.). *Wing area:* 159·3 sq. ft. (14·80 sq. m.). *Take-off weight:* 1,839 lb. (834 kg.). *Maximum speed:* 136·7 m.p.h. (220 km./hr.) at sea level. *Service ceiling:* 21,982 ft. (6,700 m.). *Endurance:* 1 hr. 30 min.

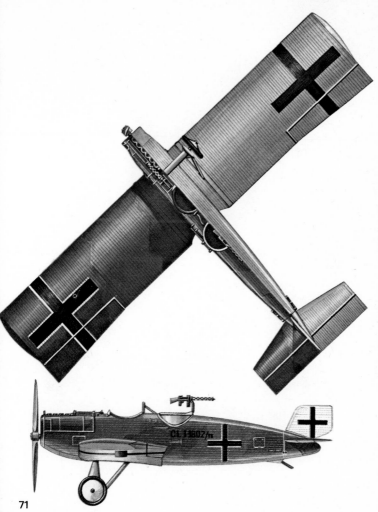

71

Junkers CL.I of the Imperial German Military Aviation Service, summer 1918. *Engine:* One 180 h.p. Mercedes D.IIIa water-cooled in-line. *Span:* 39 ft. 6⅜ in. (12·05 m.). *Length:* 25 ft. 11 in. (7·90 m.). *Wing area:* 251·9 sq. ft. (23·40 sq m.). *Take-off weight:* 2,326 lb. (1,055 kg.). *Maximum speed:* 105 m.p.h. (169 km./hr.) at sea level. *Service ceiling:* approx. 19,685 ft. (6,000 m.). *Endurance:* 2 hr. 0 min.

HANSA-BRANDENBURG CC (Germany)

72

Hansa-Brandenburg CC flown by Lt. Gottfried Banfield of the Austro-Hungarian Navy, 1917. *Engine:* One 185 h.p. Austro-Daimler water-cooled in-line. *Span:* 30 ft. 6⅛ in. (9·30 m.). *Length:* 30 ft. 0¼ in. (9·15 m.). *Wing area:* 285·2 sq. ft. (26·50 sq. m.). *Take-off weight:* 2,604 lb (1,181 kg.). *Maximum speed:* 99·4 m.p.h. (160 km./hr.) at sea level. *Service ceiling:* approx. 10,825 ft. (3,300 m.). *Endurance:* 3 hr. 30 min.

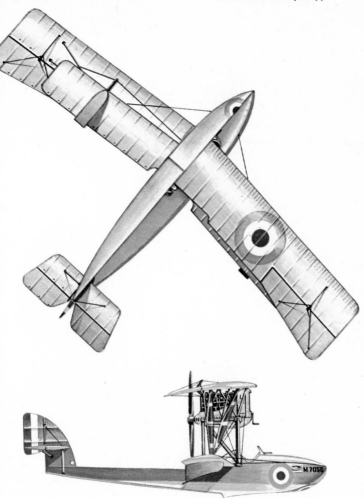

73

Macchi M.5 of the *Regia Marina Italiana, ca* early 1918. *Engine:* One 160
h.p. Isotta-Fraschini V-4B water-cooled Vee-type. *Span:* 39 ft. 0½ in. (11·90
m.). *Length:* 26 ft. 5⅓ in. (8·06 m.). *Wing area:* 301·4 sq. ft. (28·00 sq.
m.). *Take-off weight:* 2,138 lb (970 kg.). *Maximum speed:* 117·4 m.p.h.
(189 km./hr.) at sea level. *Service ceiling:* 15,091 ft. (4,600 m.). *Endurance:*
3 hr. 0 min.

ALBATROS W.4 (Germany)

74

Albatros W.4 from an Imperial German Navy seaplane base on the Flanders coast, *ca.* autumn 1917. *Engine:* One 160 h.p. Mercedes D.III water-cooled in-line. *Span:* 31 ft. 2⅙ in. (9·50 m.). *Length:* 27 ft. 10⅔ in. (8·50 m.). *Wing area:* 340·1 sq. ft. (31·60 sq. m.). *Take-off weight:* 2,359 lb. (1,070 kg.). *Maximum speed:* 99·4 m.p.h. (160 km./hr.) at sea level. *Service ceiling:* 9,843 ft. (3,000 m.). *Endurance:* 3 hr. 0 min.

RUMPLER 6B (Germany)

75

Rumpler 6B-1 of the Imperial German Navy, spring 1917. *Engine:* One 160 h.p. Mercedes D.III water-cooled in-line. *Span:* 39 ft. 6¾ in. (12·05 m.). *Length:* 30 ft. 10⅛ in. (9·40 m.). *Wing area:* 387·5 sq. ft. (36·00 sq. m.). *Maximum take-off weight:* 2,513 lb. (1,140 kg.). *Maximum speed:* 95·1 m.p.h. (153 km./hr.) at sea level. *Service ceiling:* 16,404 ft. (5,000 m.). *Endurance:* 4 hr. 0 min.

HANSA-BRANDENBURG KDW (Germany)

76

Hansa-Brandenburg KDW of the Imperial German Navy, February 1917. *Engine:* One 150 h.p. Benz Bz.III water-cooled in-line. *Span:* 30 ft. 2¼ in. (9·20 m.). *Length:* 26 ft. 3 in. (8·00 m.). *Wing area:* 313·8 sq. ft. (29·15 sq. m.). *Take-off weight:* 2,293 lb. (1,040 kg.). *Maximum speed:* 106·9 m.p.h. (172 km./hr.) at sea level. *Service ceiling:* approx. 13,123 ft. (4,000 m.). *Endurance:* 2 hr. 30 min.

HANSA-BRANDENBURG W.12 (Germany)

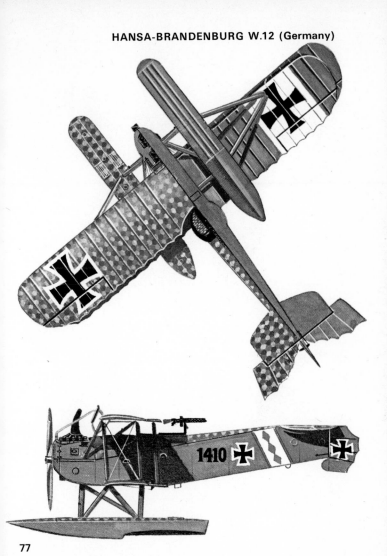

77

Hansa-Brandenburg W.12 of the Imperial German Navy, late summer 1917. *Engine:* One 150 h.p. Benz Bz.III water-cooled in-line. *Span:* 36 ft. 9 in. (11·20 m.). *Length:* 31 ft. 7⅞ in. (9·65 m.). *Wing area:* 389·7 sq. ft. (36·20 sq. m.). *Take-off weight:* 3,230 lb (1,465 kg.). *Maximum speed:* 99·4 m.p.h. (160 km./hr.) at sea level. *Service ceiling:* 16,404 ft. (5,000 m.). *Endurance:* 3 hr. 30 min.

CURTISS N-9 (U.S.A.)

78

Curtiss N-9 of a U.S. Navy training establishment, *ca.* late 1918. *Engine:* One 100 h.p. Curtiss OXX-6 water-cooled Vee-type. *Span:* 53 ft. 3¾ in. (16·25 m.). *Length:* 30 ft. 10 in. (9·40 m.). *Wing area:* 496·0 sq. ft. (46·08 sq. m.). *Take-off weight:* 2,410 lb. (1,093 kg.). *Maximum speed:* 70 m.p.h. (112·7 km./hr.) at sea level. *Service ceiling:* approx. 9,000 ft. (2,743 m.). *Endurance:* approx. 2 hr. 0 min.

SABLATNIG SF2 (Germany)

79

L.V.G.-built SF2 of the Imperial German Navy, late 1916. *Engine:* One 160 h.p. Mercedes D.III water-cooled in-line. *Span:* 60 ft. 9½ in. (18·53 m.). *Length:* 31 ft. 3¼ in. (9·53 m.). *Wing area:* 602·8 sq. ft. (56·00 sq. m.). *Take-off weight:* 3,741 lb. (1,697 kg.). *Maximum speed:* 80·8 m.p.h. (130 km./hr.) at sea level. *Service ceiling:* approx. 12,500 ft. (3,800 m.). *Endurance:* approx. 4 hr. 0 min.

HANSA-BRANDENBURG W.29 (Germany)

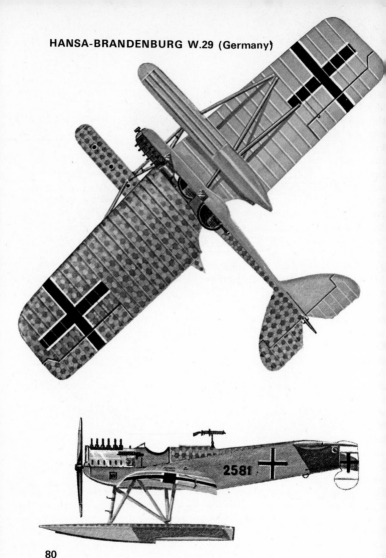

80

Hansa-Brandenburg W.29 of the Imperial German Navy, autumn 1918. *Engine:* One 150 h.p. Benz Bz.III water-cooled in-line. *Span:* 44 ft. 3½ in. (13·50 m.). *Length:* 30 ft. 6¼ in. (9·30 m.). *Wing area:* 340·1 sq. ft. (31·60 sq. m.). *Take-off weight:* 3,131 lb. (1,420 kg.). *Maximum speed:* 105·6 m.p.h. (170 km./hr.) at sea level. *Service ceiling:* over 9,843 ft. (3,000 m.). *Endurance:* 4 hr. 0 min.

Farman MF.7 and MF.11

These were both Maurice Farman designs, although Maurice and Henry Farman factories built the later machines. The MF.7, originally known as the Type 1913 from the year of its appearance, was already in service with British and French forces a year or more before the war. It was a nacelle-and-tail-boom pusher, with the nacelle 'resting' on the lower wing and a biplane tail with twin rudders mounted between. The long, curved outriggers bearing the front elevator soon earned it the nickname 'Longhorn' in British service. R.F.C. Squadrons 2, 4 and 6 were equipped with the MF.7 (British designation S.7), and a number served with the R.F.C.'s Naval Wing. The type equipped seven *escadrilles* of the French *Aviation Militaire* and some units of the Belgian *Aviation Militaire*. In the early months of the war the MF.7 was used widely for observation flights until MF.11s arrived in May 1915. Most early British 'Longhorns' were built by the Aircraft Manufacturing Co.; subsequent batches by Brush (fifty), Robey (seventeen) and Phoenix Dynamo (thirty). The Robey- and Phoenix-built aircraft were powered by 75 h.p. Rolls-Royce Hawk engines, but most MF.7s had a 70 h.p. Renault.

The MF.11, a 1914 design, was built in far greater numbers than the MF.7, equipping thirty-seven French *escadrilles*, Nos. 1, 2, 4, 9, 16 and 30 Squadrons of the R.F.C. on the Western Front and other R.F.C./R.N.A.S. units in Mesopotamia, the Dardanelles and the Aegean. The MF.11 had upper- and lower-wing ailerons, and its nacelle was mounted mid-way between the wings; a single tailplane bore twin fins and rudders. There were no front elevator or skids, and the MF11 inevitably became the 'Shorthorn'. Usual powerplant was the 100 h.p. Renault, though a variety of alternatives were fitted. While the MF.7 had been unarmed, the MF.11 was employed on reconnaissance and bombing duties, the observer at first occupying the rear cockpit with a hand-held machine-gun. A later version, the MF.11*bis*, had the observer sitting in front with a forward-firing Lewis or Hotchkiss gun; a variation was to mount the gun over the top wing, the observer standing up to train the gun to the front or rear. The R.N.A.S. had some ninety S.11s (British designation), and one made the first night bombing raid of the war. This was on 21 December 1914 against German gun emplacements near Ostend, the aircraft carrying eighteen 16 lb. H.E.R.L. bombs. Some R.N.A.S. 'Shorthorns' were operated as twin-float seaplanes, a practice also followed in Italy, where French-built Farmans preceded licence construction of the MF.11 by S.I.A. with 100 h.p. Fiat A-10 or Colombo engines. Italian-built MF.11s were supplied to at least twenty-four *squadriglie*, and others with 80 h.p. Gnome engines to training establishments. On the Western Front the MF.11 began to be replaced in autumn 1915, but for some time after this it and the MF.7 continued to be used widely and successfully as training aircraft.

Some Farmans also served with the Imperial Russian Air Service.

2 Airco D.H.1 and D.H.1A

The D.H.1 was the third of Geoffrey de Havilland's designs to be built, earlier ventures being an unsuccessful machine which he built himself in 1909 and the more successful F.E.1 of 1910. The F.E.1 was later rebuilt as the F.E.2, and the Airco D.H.1 followed a similar 2-seat pusher layout. It was intended for fighter and reconnaissance duties, with the observer occupying the front cockpit and provided with a forward-firing machine-gun.

The prototype D.H.1 was completed at Hendon early in 1915, where it was flown by de Havilland himself. It had been intended to power the D.H.1 with the 120 h.p. Beardmore engine, but these were in comparatively short supply and were more urgently required for the Royal Aircraft Factory's F.E.2b and R.E.5. The prototype was therefore fitted with a 70 h.p. Renault engine, with which, despite the much lower power, the aircraft's performance was still creditable. An order for one hundred D.H.1s was placed with Savages Ltd. of Kings Lynn, a company with no previous aircraft manufacturing experience. These differed from the prototype in having dual controls, a slightly modified nacelle, reinforced bracing wires and an undercarriage of simplified construction. As the supply of Beardmore engines improved, these were used instead of the Renaults, resulting in an increase of some 10 per cent in the fuel load and nearly

300 lb. (136 kg.) in the maximum weight. Despite this, the D.H.1A, a the Beardmore-engined version wa known, was some 8 m.p.h. (12·8 km hr.) faster than the D.H.1, and coul climb to 4,000 ft. (1,219 m.) in 8 minutes compared with 11¼ minute taken by the D.H.1. It also prove to be more responsive and mano euvrable than the contemporar F.E.2b.

Although the entire productio quantity was built, only seventy three D.H.1/1As were issued to th R.F.C. These were employed mainl on Home Defence and, later, train ing duties in the United Kingdom although one squadron, No. 14 made limited use of six D.H.1As i Palestine from summer 1916. Em ployed largely as escorts, they wer still in service in spring 1917. Som British-based aircraft survived unti 1918, but all were withdrawn from service some months before th Armistice.

3 Airco D.H.2

The D.H.2 was essentially a scaled down version of the 2-seat D.H.1. I was a single-seat pusher whose proto type, 4732, appeared in spring 191 powered by a 100 h.p. Gnom Monosoupape. A single Lewis gu was installed on a pivot mounting t the port side of the cockpit. In Jul 1915 it was sent to France for opera tional trials with No. 5 Squadro R.F.C., but was brought down i enemy territory on 9 August.

Despite this unpropitious start t its career, the D.H.2 was ordered fo quantity production and the firs deliveries were made in late 1915 t

No. 24 Squadron. This unit went to France in February 1916 with twelve D.H.2s, the first-ever squadron to be equipped with single-seat fighters. The Lewis gun was now situated centrally in the prow, on a free mounting that enabled it to be traversed from left to right or elevated upward or downward; in general, pilots found this mounting too wobbly and often improvised a method of securing it in a forward-firing position so that, by aiming the whole aeroplane, they also aimed the gun. They found the D.H.2 tricky to handle at first, but when they had mastered it discovered that it was rugged and highly manoeuvrable. The Monosoupape was retained, despite its propensity for shedding cylinders in mid-air; at least one D.H.2 was fitted experimentally with a 110 h.p. Le Rhône 9J.

The D.H.2 possibly did more than any other Allied aeroplane to overcome the Fokker threat, which appeared over the Western Front at about the time the D.H.2 was undergoing its early trials. No. 24 Squadron scored its first aerial victory on 2 April 1916 and claimed its first Fokker on 25 April, after which crews attacked the Fokkers with gusto. Later that spring Nos. 29 and 32 Squadrons were fully equipped with D.H.2s, and other squadrons to use them included Nos. 5, 11 and 18. Altogether about two-thirds of the four hundred D.H.2s built were sent to France. Major L. W. B. Rees, commanding No. 32 Squadron, was awarded the V.C. for his single-handed attack in a D.H.2 on ten German 2-seaters on 1 July 1916.

By the autumn the D.H.2 was being outflown and outgunned by the new German biplane fighters, and on 23 November 1916 Major L. G. Hawker, V.C., D.S.O., the ebullient C.O. of No. 24 Squadron, was shot down by von Richthofen flying an Albatros D.II. Withdrawal of the D.H.2 from France started in March 1917, and was completed in June. A somewhat longer operational life was enjoyed by D.H.2s serving with the 5th Wing, No. 11 Squadron and 'X' Flight in Palestine, and with 'A' Flight of 47 Squadron and a joint R.F.C./ R.N.A.S. fighter squadron in Macedonia. (The Admiralty evaluated one D.H.2, but decided not to adopt the type and transferred the machine to the R.F.C.) Two D.H.2s were tried out in 1917 at Home Defence units, but their performance was below that necessary to cope with the Zeppelin raiders. After withdrawal from front-line duties, many were allocated to training units in the United Kingdom, where they served until 1918.

4 Royal Aircraft Factory F.E.2b and F.E.2d

Had it been possible to get the F.E.2b more quickly into service, it is arguable that the Fokker monoplane fighters would never have achieved the supremacy that they did. The original F.E.2a (2864) was probably designed in the summer of 1914; an initial batch of twelve were ordered from the Royal Aircraft Factory, the first flying on 26 January 1915. A 2-seat pusher, this aircraft was powered by a 100 h.p.

Green engine, and to facilitate production and servicing had identical outer wing sections to the B.E.2c. The Green engine proved unsatisfactory, and all aircraft were subsequently modified to accept the 120 h.p. Beardmore, first flying with this engine on 16 March 1915. Deliveries began in May, arriving in France later that month with No. 6 Squadron R.F.C. Armament consisted of a forward-firing 0·303 in. Lewis gun, on a movable mounting in the front cockpit. Production of the F.E.2b, a modified and somewhat simplified version, began in the autumn of 1915, and these aircraft became operational at around the turn of the year. Throughout the spring and summer of 1916 the F.E.2b flew and fought well, later aircraft benefiting from 160 h.p. Beardmore engines. By the autumn they were outclassed as fighters by the German Albatroses, and in November No. 18 Squadron introduced the F.E.2b to a new role – night bombing. For this it carried one 230 lb. or three 112 lb. bombs. Other F.E.2b squadrons subsequently converted to a bombing role, and new squadrons were also formed for the purpose, the first being No. 100, which began operations in March 1917. The type remained in R.F.C. service on the Western Front until the end of the war, equipping sixteen squadrons and one flight. Five Home Defence units had F.E.2bs, but its poor ceiling and rate of climb rendered it comparatively ineffective as a night fighter.

In 1916 the Factory converted two F.E.2bs into F.E.2cs, one of these having the crew position reversed to facilitate night landings. This version was not developed, but the F.E.2c designation was applied in 1918 to some night bomber F.E.2bs with a similar seating arrangement. From spring 1916 the F.E.2bs in service were joined by the improved F.E.2d in which a 250 h.p. Rolls-Royce Eagle engine raised the speed to 94 m.p.h. (151·3 km/hr.). Official figures aver that one thousand nine hundred and thirty-nine F.E.2bs were built, but known serial allocations only account for one thousand four hundred and eighty-four of these. The F.E.2b was subcontracted to at least five other manufacturers, principal contributors being Boulton & Paul and G. and J. Weir. Three hundred F.E.2ds were ordered from Boulton & Paul, and a further eighty-five were built by the Factory. A few F.E.2bs were used for ground strafing, with a 1-pdr. Vickers gun in place of the front Lewis.

5 Royal Aircraft Factory F.E.8

The absence of an interrupter gear, to permit an effective forward-firing armament to be combined with the superior performance inherent in a tractor biplane layout, inhibited too many British fighters for too much of the 1914–18 war. Among the victims of this situation was the F.E.8. Drawn up in mid-1915 by J. Kenworthy of the Royal Aircraft Factory, it was a good design in itself; but a year was to pass before it reached the Front, by which time its opponents were the sleek, fast, twin-gunned Albatroses. Its career was hampered still further by its temperamental Gnome Monosoupape engine.

When originally completed in October 1915, the prototype F.E.8 (7456) was unarmed, but shortly afterwards a stripped-down Lewis gun was installed semi-enclosed in the lower front part of the nacelle. A second machine, 7457, underwent service trials in France in December 1915 (the first aircraft had by then been damaged in a crash), and production commenced early in 1916. The Monosoupape was retained as standard power-plant, although experimental installations were made of 110 h.p. Clerget and Le Rhône rotaries. The major F.E.8 contractor was the Darracq Motor Engineering Co., which built two hundred and forty-five; a further fifty were completed by Vickers at Weybridge. On production F.E.8s the semi-buried Lewis was exchanged for a more conventional and more convenient location in the front of the cockpit, with a tray on each side of the nacelle to hold additional ammunition drums.

The F.E.8 was apparently issued to only three R.F.C. squadrons: No. 29 in June 1916, No. 40 in August and No. 41 in the following October. As already observed, the type's obsolete layout, poor performance and inadequate armament made it easy prey to fighters of the Albatros's quality. The helplessness of the lumbering pusher type of fighter against late-war German single-seaters was demonstrated emphatically on 9 March 1917, when Albatros D.IIIs from von Richthofen's *Jasta* 11 destroyed four and damaged another four of a formation of nine F.E.8s, and shortly after this No. 40 Squadron replaced its F.E.8s with Nieuport 17s. Those of No. 41 Squadron served until replaced with D.H.5s in July. Serial numbers were allocated for two F.E.8s for the R.N.A.S., but these were not taken up.

6 Vickers F.B.5 and F.B.9

Vickers Ltd was one of the first companies to recognise the potentialities of the aeroplane for waging, and not simply observing, war. At the 1913 Aero Show at Olympia it exhibited the Type 18 'Destroyer', a 2-seat biplane with a water-cooled Wolseley pusher engine and a free-firing, belt-fed Maxim gun in the nose. This was later classified E.F.B.1 (Experimental Fighting Biplane No. 1), and further developed via the E.F.B.2 (Type 18A) and E.F.B.3 (Type 18B), and in December 1913 six modified 18Bs were ordered for the R.N.A.S. as Vickers Type 30s, but before delivery the design was further improved as the E.F.B.5 (the E.F.B.4 being an unbuilt project) and the contract was taken over by the War Office for the R.F.C.

Production F.B.5s differed in having a more manageable drum-fed Lewis gun in place of the heavier Maxim, a Gnome Monosoupape engine, smaller nacelle, rectangular horizontal tail surfaces and a modified rudder. They were at first allocated to squadrons in small numbers only. The first unit to be fully equipped with them – and hence the first specialised fighter squadron ever to be formed – was No. 11 Squadron, which began to receive F.B.5s in February 1915 and arrived in France with them in July. Here they did useful work for several months, both in aerial fighting and in ground strafing with a light load of bombs. Never very fast, the F.B.5 took nearly half an hour to reach its modest ceiling of 9,000 ft. (2,743 m.) and was up against the Fokker tractor monoplane fighters with their synchronised guns by the time No. 18 Squadron arrived in France with its F.B.5s in November. Nevertheless, the type remained in service until July 1916, No. 11 Squadron latterly experimenting with a twin-Lewis installation. An improved version, the F.B.9, appeared in December 1915. This had round-tipped wings of 2 ft. 9 in. (0·84 m.) less span, rounded tailplane and a fully rotatable Lewis gun on a ball-and-socket mounting in the prow of a more streamlined nacelle. (The F.B.5 had been dubbed 'Gunbus'; the F.B.9 therefore became the 'Streamline Gunbus'.) The Monosoupape was retained, though a few F.B.9s may have been fitted with 110 h.p. Le Rhône 9 Js.

Production was undertaken chiefly at Vickers' Crayford works, where one hundred and fifteen F.B.5s and forty-five F.B.9s were built; a further fifty F.B.9s were completed at the Weybridge factory. Licence production of ninety-nine F.B.5s was begun by S.A. Darracq at Suresnes in France, but some of these are believed to have been completed as F.B.9s. Twelve F.B.5s were built under licence in Denmark in 1917–18. At least twenty-seven of the early F.B.5s were originally earmarked for the R.N.A.S. as Admiralty Type 32s, but thirteen are known to have been taken over by the R.F.C. and little operational use of the type was made by the Navy. The F.B.9's operational career was fairly uneventful, except for a brief appearance at the Battle of the Somme, and from autumn 1916 both these and the surviving F.B.5s were used chiefly for training duties.

7 Spad A2

The reluctance of British and French authorities to back the development of an interrupter mechanism, to enable a machine-gun to be fired between the revolving blades of a propeller, forced designers to pursue alternative methods of providing a forward-firing armament. The most commonplace solution was the 'pusher' engine layout, but a more freakish approach was that typified by the Royal Aircraft Factory's B.E.9 and the Spad A2. The latter was evolved under Louis Bechereau, technical director of the Spad company, and was in essence a tractor biplane with an additional front nacelle, intended to give the forward crew member the maximum field of view and of fire. Powerplant consisted of an 80 h.p. Le Rhône 9 C in the A1, the first version to appear. This was a 2-seater, with the pilot sitting behind a wide rectangular cut-out in the trailing edge and the observer/gunner in a pointed nacelle ahead of the propeller. When access to the engine was required, the nacelle pivoted forward and downward from the axle, being attached at other times to the top-wing framework by steel tubes, and by an extension of the propeller shaft turning in a ball race at the back of the nacelle. On test, the A1 achieved a speed of 152 km/hr. (94·4 m.p.h.). First production version was the A2, powered by a 110 h.p. Le Rhône 9 J. The first A2 was flown on 21 May 1915, and a further ninety-nine were built – forty-two for the French *Aviation Militaire* and fifty-seven for the Imperial Russian Air Service. Russian A2s later had their wheeled landing gear replaced by skis.

As might have been foreseen, the A2 was heartily disliked by the crews that had to fly in it. Its layout seriously hampered the efficiency of the propeller, the pilot's view forward was obstructed by the observer and his gun, and the A2 must have been most difficult to land. The nacelle achieved its purpose in providing the observer with an excellent field of view, but his pylon-mounted Lewis gun was capable of only limited movement, and only a semicircular wire mesh guard separated him from the propeller at his back. In the event of a nose-over landing he was almost certain to be seriously injured.

Not surprisingly, the A2's operational career with the *Aviation Militaire* was brief. The Russian Air Service, because of a general shortage of equipment, was obliged to retain its A2s somewhat longer, and this was no doubt the reason for its

acceptance of ten A4s, a development of the A2 which first flew on 22 February 1916. A prototype A3 was completed, with dual controls and a machine-gun in each cockpit; each crew member could act as either pilot or gunner. No production of this model was undertaken. Final prototype was the A5, produced in 1916 for the Military Competition; this resembled the A4 but had a Renault 8 Fg engine.

8 Hannover CL types

In early 1917 the *Flugzeugmeisterei* introduced a new CL category, for 2-seat aircraft weighing less than 750 kg. (1,653 lb) empty. The first in this category by the Hannoversche Waggonfabrik A.G. was designed by Hermann Dorner and designated CL.II. It was a small, compact biplane with a 180 h.p. Argus As.III engine and wings resembling the 'Libellule' of the later Rumpler C types. A feature of the design, which remained unique among German single-engined aircraft of the war period, was the biplane tail unit.

Production CL.IIs had increased lower-wing dihedral and a more rounded upper tailplane. Four hundred and thirty-nine were built, but it is not certain if this includes CL.IIs built by L.F.G. (Roland) and designated CL.IIa. The CL.IIs entered service from December 1917, armed with a single, centrally mounted Spandau front gun and a Parabellum gun on a ring mounting for the observer. Because of the narrow gap between fuselage and upper wing, the pilot had an excellent view forward and upward, and the narrower lower wings extended his view below. The short tailplane span, made possible by using a compound assembly, gave the observer a better-than-usual field of fire to the rear. The CL.II was followed by the CL.III, which had a 160 h.p. Mercedes D.III and overhung ailerons. Because of the demand for Mercedes for fighter aircraft, only eighty CL.IIIs were built; a return was then made to the As.III, with which the aircraft became the CL.IIIa. Five hundred and thirty-seven CL.IIIas were built.

The 'Hannoveranas' were good flying machines and highly manoeuvrable; they were also very strong, and could absorb a great deal of battle damage. Their climb rate was not outstanding, but they possessed an excellent ceiling which enabled them to fulfil their original function of escort fighter. They were equally nimble at low altitudes, and were widely used from spring 1918 for ground attack, carrying stick grenades in small racks on the fuselage sides abreast of the observer's cockpit.

About fifty CL.Vs were built during 1918, some with compound tails and others with a single tailplane. These were powered by 185 h.p. B.M.W.IIIa engines, which raised the speed to 185 km/hr. (114·9 m.p.h.) and the ceiling to an outstanding 9,000 m. (29,528 ft.). In common with most late-war aircraft designed around this powerplant, the CL.V probably saw little, if any, operational service. Another 1918 variant was the C.IV (sometimes mistakenly called the CL.IV).

This was a typical C type, but only one or two were built. It was based on the CL.II/III, but was larger, had simplified bracing and a 245 h.p. Maybach Mb.IV. Experimental conversions of the CL.IIIa were the CL.IIIb (190 h.p. N.A.G.) and the CL.IIIc (extended, 2-bay wings).

9 Halberstadt CL.II and CL.IV

Early in 1917 a new class of German 2-seater was introduced: the CL category, a smaller, lighter version of the C type intended to provide protective escort for their heavier brethren and support for the ground forces. The first aircraft to be produced in this category was the Halberstadt CL.II, a neat, compact biplane with its crew seated in a long communal cockpit. Armament consisted of one or two 7·92 mm. synchronised Spandau guns on top of the front fuselage, and a Parabellum gun of similar calibre on an elevated ring mounting in the rear; four or five 10 kg. mortar bombs or a number of small grenades were carried in trays attached to the fuselage on either side of the observer.

The CL.II entered service in mid-1917, quickly making its presence felt. On 6 September twenty-four CL.IIs, against virtually no air opposition, wrought havoc among Allied troops crossing the Somme bridges. Following this action, increasing use was made of the CL.II in the close support role, and it was largely due to aircraft of this type that the Germans were able to make such an effective counter-offensive at the Battle of Cambrai on 30 November. The expansion of the German *Schlachtstaffeln* (Battle Flights) was made largely with the CL.II and the later CL.IV, and by the spring offensive of March 1918 most of the 38 *Schlastas* then in existence, each with an establishment for six aircraft, were equipped with Halberstadt CL types. They had a marked effect upon the morale of the Allied troops in the trenches who were subjected to their attacks. After the failure of the March offensive they reverted mainly to a defensive role, although some continued to be used for nuisance raids by night on Allied airfields. Other duties included the interception of Allied night bombers and defensive support of the ground troops.

A few examples were built of the CL.IIa, with a 185 h.p. B.M.W. IIIa engine in a more streamlined nose; but the only other major variant was the CL.IV, which appeared early in 1918. This retained the Mercedes D.III, though in a blunter cowling, the fuselage was some 2½ feet (0·76 m.) shorter, and had a wider-span tailplane and a more rounded fin and rudder. The CL.IV had much the same overall performance as the CL.II, but it was more manoeuvrable. Production of the CL.II was shared by Bayerische Flugzeug-Werke, and of the CL.IV by L.F.G. (Roland).

10 **Packard-Le Père LUSAC-11**
The A.E.F. in Europe was equipped for most of its operational service with French-designed and built combat aircraft, while production within the United States was centred chiefly on training types. However, one combat type that did emerge was the LUSAC-11. This was designed by Capitaine G. Le Père of the French aviation mission to the United States, its designation indicating Le Père U.S. Army Combat.

The LUSAC-11 was designed as an escort and patrol fighter, and the first prototype (42128) was handed over to the U.S. Army Air Service in September 1918. Both this and the second machine had a wing span of 39 ft. 0 in. (11·89 m.). One thousand and twenty production machines with increased wing span and 425 h.p. Liberty 12 engines were ordered from the Packard Motor Car Co. at Detroit, but only twenty-five of these had been completed by the end of the war. The remaining nine hundred and ninety-five, plus three thousand four hundred and ninety-five ordered on three subsequent contracts, were cancelled after the Armistice. Armament of the LUSAC-11 comprised two synchronised forward-firing 0·30-in. Marlin machine-guns on the starboard side of the front fuselage, and twin Lewis guns on a Scarff ring mounting in the rear cockpit. Of incidental interest is the fact that the LUSAC-11 was the first U.S. production aeroplane to have a supercharged engine.

Only the first two production aircraft had reached France, for service trials, before the Armistice. They proved to be rugged, fast and manoeuvrable, with a 20,000 ft. (6,096 m.) ceiling to which they could climb in some 41 minutes. Subject to the elimination of fuel supply and engine cooling problems which gave a little early trouble, the LUSAC-11 would have been a valuable combat type had the war continued.

Three examples were completed of a slightly heavier version, the LUSAC-21, in which 420 h.p. Bugatti 16 engines were installed. Performance was inferior to the Liberty-engined model, and its development was not pursued. Single examples were delivered in November 1918 and January 1919 of the LUSAGH-11 and LUSAGH-21, these being Liberty- and Bugatti-engined models for ground attack (GH = Ground Harassment) with a shorter fuselage and increased wing span. The LUSAO-11 was a 3-seat observation triplane, two of which were completed early in 1919, also powered by Liberty 12 engines. A variant of the LUSAC-11 (possibly the LUSAC-25) was projected with a 300 h.p. Hispano-Suiza engine, but was never built.

11 Bristol F.2A and F.2B

The Bristol Fighter was the most successful of F. S. Barnwell's many designs for the British and Colonial Aeroplane Co. It originated as the R.2A (120 h.p. Beardmore) and R.2B (150 h.p. Hispano-Suiza) 2-seat reconnaissance biplanes, which were further developed into the F.2A fighter. Two prototype F.2As were built, one with a 190 h.p. Rolls-Royce Falcon flying on 9 September 1916 and the other, with a Hispano-Suiza, on 25 October.

Fifty Falcon-engined F.2As were built, armed with a centrally mounted Vickers gun synchronised with Constantinesco gear and a single Lewis on a Scarff ring mounting in the rear cockpit. Deliveries began in December 1916, and the first F.2A squadron (No. 48) arrived in France with them in March 1917. At first they were flown like the previous 2-seaters, orientated around the observer's gun as the primary weapon, and losses were heavy. After a few weeks new tactics were evolved and, when flown as a front-gun fighter, the Bristol soon achieved a remarkable success. Many hundreds more Bristol Fighters were now on order, these being F.2Bs with wider-span tailplanes, modified lower centre-sections and an even better view from the front cockpit. The first hundred and fifty F.2Bs were powered by Falcon I engines, the next fifty by 220 h.p. Falcon IIs and subsequent batches were scheduled to have the superb 275 h.p. Falcon III. In July 1917 the War Office ordered eight hundred more F.2Bs to re-equip all R.F.C. fighter reconnaissance and corps reconnaissance squadrons. The supply of Falcons could not keep pace with production on this scale, and several alternative units were investigated. Of these the 200 h.p. Sunbeam Arab was the most widely used, although far from satisfactory.

Re-equipment of squadrons in France with F.2Bs quickly gathered pace from the summer of 1917, and by spring 1918 the fighter had established such a reputation that enemy fighters could be relied upon not to attack more than two Bristols at a time. The F.2B eventually served with six Western Front squadrons: Nos. 11, 20, 22, 48, 62 and 88. In Palestine, F.2Bs served with No. 67 (Australian) Squadron; a few were also used by 111 Squadron, and two were allocated to transport T.E. Lawrence between General Allenby's headquarters and the Arab guerrilla forces. No. 139 Squadron in Italy also fought with F.2Bs, while at home they served with Home Defence Squadrons 33, 36, 39, 76 and 141.

Under wartime contracts more than five thousand two hundred and fifty Bristol Fighters were ordered; three thousand one hundred and one are known to have been accepted by R.F.C./R.A.F. units up to November 1918. Following the delivery of two pattern aircraft in 1917–18, plans were made for large-scale production in the United States, but despite all advice to the contrary, American authorities insisted on installing the utterly unsuitable 400 h.p. Liberty 12, with disastrous results; and contracts for Curtiss to build two thousand F.2Bs (the first of which flew on 5 March 1918) under the designation O-1 were cancelled after only twenty-seven had been built. The Bristol Fighter remained in post-war R.A.F. service as a standard type until 1932) see the *Fighters Between The Wars* volume in this series). Civil conversions of wartime machines appeared in 1919, including a coupé and a 2-seat open tourer version with a 230 h.p. Armstrong Siddeley Puma.

12 Curtiss JN series

The 'Jenny' was produced to a U.S. Army requirement, issued in 1914, for a tractor biplane trainer. The Curtiss Aeroplane and Motor Co. engaged B. D. Thomas of Sopwith Aviation, who designed the Model J powered by a 90 h.p. Curtiss OX-5 engine; and evolved a design of its own, the Model N, which was generally similar except for large between-wing ailerons. The best features of each were built into a new model known as the JN, which, with minor improvements, was evaluated as the JN-1 by the U.S. Army and Navy. An Army order followed in 1915 for ten JN-2s. Nine of these had equal-span wings with ailerons top and bottom; the other had unequal span and top-wing ailerons only. In these early trainers the ailerons were actuated by a shoulder yoke worn by the pilot, who leaned in the direction that he wanted his aircraft to go.

First major version was the JN-3 primary trainer, with conventional aileron controls and a fixed fin. At least eighty-six JN-3s were built by Curtiss in the United States, and another eighteen by its Canadian factory; ninety-seven were delivered to the R.N.A.S. In the second half of 1916 the U.S. Army ordered ninety-four similar JN-4s and these were followed by the first JN-4As, which had increased dihedral, ailerons on all wings and a redesigned vertical tail. In 1917 the designation JN-4 was also applied to a British-inspired JN-3 development incorporating features of the JN-4A. One thousand two hundred and sixty of these were built by Canadian Aeroplanes Ltd., and to distinguish them from U.S.-built JN-4s they were redesignated JN-4Can. Of two hundred and fifty ordered by the R.N.A.S., only one hundred and eighty were delivered, one hundred later being transferred to the R.F.C. The JN-4B was a hybrid, with JN-4 wings and a JN-4A tail. Only a few were built, but the JN-4B eventually gave rise to the N-9 seaplane (described separately). The JN-4C was experimental, using a different aerofoil wing section.

Most widely produced 'Jenny' was the JN-4D, similar to the JN-4A except in its flying controls and trailing-edge cut-outs. Two thousand seven hundred and sixty-five JN-4Ds and JN-4D-2s were completed. In 1917 a JN-4D, re-engined with a 150 h.p. Hispano-Suiza, gave rise to the JN-4H advanced trainer, of which nine hundred and twenty-nine were built. After entry into service these were subdivided into specialised training categories – e.g., bombing, gunnery, etc. They were joined by one thousand and thirty-five JN-6Hs with Wright-built Hispano As.

Over five and a half thousand Curtiss OX-powered JN-4-type machines were turned out. After the Armistice, hundreds were re-purchased by Curtiss and refurbished for the civil market, where they embarked on a second extensive career as private-owner, flying-circus and 'barnstorming' aircraft. The Hispano-powered 'Jennies' remained in U.S. Army service for several post-war years, finally being withdrawn in 1927.

13 Airco D.H.6

The D.H.6 was a 2-seat primary trainer produced to meet an urgent need for trained pilots for the R.F.C. in autumn 1916. It was functional rather than beautiful, the emphasis being on an aeroplane easy to build, fly and maintain in the field. The wings were unrelieved rectangles, all four sections of which were interchangeable, and the tailplane followed a similar pattern. The two prototypes (A5175 and A5176) featured a typical D.H.-pattern vertical tail and a round-topped rear fuselage, but on production aircraft even these curves were eliminated. The two occupants were seated in a long, communal cockpit.

Production began in January 1917, two thousand nine hundred and fifty being ordered: nine hundred from the parent company, seven hundred and fifty from Grahame-White Aviation, four hundred from Ransome, Sims and Jeffries, three hundred from Harland & Wolff, two hundred from Morgan & Co., one hundred and fifty each from the Gloucestershire Aircraft Co. and Kingsbury Aviation Co., and one hundred from Savages Ltd. Most were powered by the 90 h.p. R.A.F.1a, but several were completed with a cowled 90 h.p. Curtiss OX-5 or an 80 h.p. Renault. Performance of the D.H.6 was unspectacular, but it was extremely safe to fly – some said too safe. With the introduction of the Avro 504 as the standard British trainer late in 1917, it began to be withdrawn, but early in 1918 two hundred or so were pressed into service with the

R.N.A.S. for submarine-hunting in British coastal waters. They were flown as single-seaters, but even without an observer could only carry a maximum bomb load of 100 lb. (45·4 kg.). Thirty-four coastal flights were equipped with D.H.6s, five of them operated by the U.S. Navy. There is no record that D.H.6s claimed any U-boat victims, but their presence may have provided a useful deterrent to attacks on Allied shipping. Seventy-one D.H.6s were allocated to Home Defence units in 1918, but these were probably used only for liaison and not in anti-Zeppelin operations.

A vain attempt was made to improve performance by giving the wings slight backward stagger and reducing the size of the elevators and rudder. One Curtiss-engined machine was fitted experimentally with flotation apparatus. On 31 October 1918 there were one thousand and fifty D.H.6s on R.A.F. charge, and over fifty came on to the British civil register after the Armistice. The first, as K-100, was the first aeroplane in Britain – perhaps in the world – to carry a civil registration. Civil D.H.6s were used mostly for joy flights, some later being converted to 3-seaters.

14 Royal Aircraft Factory B.E.12

The inherent stability of the luckless B.E.2c, while a very desirable flying quality, made the aeroplane so unmanoeuvrable that it could not escape the more nimble German fighters. Yet despite the heavy losses incurred in France by B.E.2cs, an aircraft of this type (1697) was used in the summer of 1915 as the basis for the supposedly superior B.E.12. Little more was done to this airframe than to provide it with a 150 h.p. R.A.F.4 engine and to turn it into a single-seater by covering in the front cockpit.

The B.E.12 entered production in late spring 1916 and was in service with Nos. 10, 19 and 21 Squadrons in France by the end of August; by mid-September Trenchard had ordered its withdrawal. It was later reinstated as a light bomber, carrying sixteen 16 lb. or two 112 lb. bombs, but it remained vulnerable to air attack and was in fact even less manoeuvrable than the B.E.2c. In the Middle East it equipped No. 144 Squadron and two flights in Palestine; it was a little more successful in Macedonia with Nos. 17, 47 and 50 Squadrons. Six Home Defence squadrons each received a few B.E.12s, and one (from No. 37 Squadron) shot down the Zeppelin L.48 in June 1917. By this time the B.E.12 had long since been withdrawn from the Western Front, but at Home Defence units and in the Middle East a few remained in service until the Armistice.

Variants included the B.E.12a, which utilised the wing unit of the B.E.2e; the B.E.12b, which appeared in 1917, was rather better with a 200 h.p. Hispano-Suiza 8 Ac. Total orders for the B.E.12 series amounted to six hundred: five hundred from Daimler and fifty each from Coventry Ordnance Works and the Standard Motor Co. Official records show four hundred and sixty-eight B.E. 12/12as issued to R.F.C. units; at least a hundred and fifteen of the remainder were Daimler-built B.E.12bs.

The B.E.12s featured a variety of armament arrangements. Early machines entered service with a Lewis gun on either side of the cockpit on a Strange-type mounting, firing outward at an angle to clear the propeller; later aircraft had a single port-side synchronised Vickers gun, and occasionally a Lewis was mounted on the starboard side in similar fashion or on the port side to fire to the rear. Some B.E.12bs on anti-Zeppelin duty had twin Lewis guns firing forward and upward over the top wing. After spring 1918 the employment of the B.E.12 is somewhat obscure. Some may have been used for anti-submarine patrols, though it is likely that they were relegated to training duties or placed in store.

15 **Phönix D.I to D.III**

The Phönix D.I was basically a development of the Hansa-Brandenburg D.I with a more powerful engine. Various experimental machines appeared in mid-1917, none offering any significant improvement over the Brandenburg fighter, but eventually aircraft 20.16, with a 200 h.p. Austro-Daimler engine, became in its final form an effective prototype of the Phönix D.I. In autumn 1917 three batches of fifty D.Is (Series 128, 228 and 328) were ordered from Phönix, who later built another forty Series 128s for the Austro-Hungarian Navy. Army D.Is entered service in February/

March 1918, initially on escort and reconnaissance. Before being issued to *Jagdkompagnien* in May, it became necessary to reinforce the D.I's wings, which had proved subject to failure under stress. Naval D.Is entered service about June, and remained a serious threat to Italian aircraft over the Adriatic until the end of the war. Although less manoeuvrable than Allied fighters, the Phönix was a speedy machine with a good rate of climb. One serious drawback was the inaccessibility of its twin 8 mm. Schwarzlose guns. These were fully enclosed by the engine panels, firing through holes in the nose of the cowling – an admirable aerodynamic refinement, but they were completely beyond the pilot's reach in the event of all-too-frequent stoppages. The fault persisted in the D.II and D.IIa.

The D.II had the same powerplant as the D.I, but a slightly increased wing span and other changes. Three Series (122, 222 and 322) were ordered, together with a single Series (422) of the D.IIa, which had a 230 h.p. Hiero and ailerons on both pairs of wings. Little more than half of the D.II/IIas ordered were actually completed, entering service from May 1918. Before the war ended production had begun of the Phönix D.III, an improved D.IIa whose wings were rigged without dihedral, the lower wings having plain ailerons, and the guns at last moved rearward within reach of the pilot. Two prototypes were built of the D.IV, outwardly similar but actually an entirely new design having an oval fuselage and increased vertical tail area.

In 1919, after evaluating the D.III prototype (J41), the Royal Swedish Army Aviation purchased seventeen D.IIIs from Phönix. These were originally known in Sweden as Phönix 122s, suggesting that they were laid down as D.IIs but completed as D.IIIs. A further ten D.IIIs were completed by the Swedish Army workshops at Malmen in 1924, having 185 h.p. B.M.W. IIIa engines since Austrian powerplants were no longer available. Swedish D.IIIs could be fitted with ski undercarriages during the winter. With the formation of the *Flygvapnet* in July 1926, nine Phönix 122s (then redesignated J 1) were in service with F3 Wing; they remained, latterly with F5 on communications and training duties, until 1930, and one was still carrying out meteorological flights as late as 1936. During their Swedish service some D.IIIs had large aerofoil-section fuel tanks on the upper wings, and increased vertical tail area.

16 Hansa-Brandenburg D.I

Designed by Heinkel early in 1916, the prototype of the aircraft that went into production as the Hansa-Brandenburg D.I was powered by a 160 h.p. Mercedes D.III engine and was given the nickname *Spinne* (Spider). This may have been a reference to the then unique form of interplane bracing, consisting of four small V-struts joined together in a 'star' between each pair of wings. The D.I was not one of

Heinkel's better efforts, but it was employed operationally by the Austro-Hungarian Air Service on a fairly wide scale when little else was available.

The D.I was ugly and ungainly, with a deep nose whose depth was further accentuated by a radiator mounted directly on top, effectively filling in the gap between the engine and the top wing. The cowling was shaped so that the pilot could see forward along either side of the cylinder block, but his view must have been restricted on the starboard side by the exhaust manifold. With the cockpit roughly in line with the lower trailing edge, and only a small cut-out in the top wing, the view upward and downward must also have left much to be desired. The D.I was armed with a non-synchronised 8 mm. Schwarzlose gun which seemed to have been added as an afterthought, for it was mounted in a narrow casing above the top wing, where it added to the aerodynamic drag and was completely inaccessible to the pilot during flight.

Production began late in the summer of 1916, deliveries starting in the autumn. The D.I was built in two versions: forty-eight Series 28, built by Phönix with 160 h.p. Austro-Daimler engines, and another forty-eight similarly-powered Series 65.5, built by Brandenburg. Several accidents among early aircraft in service, due to inadequate lateral control, resulted in Phönix adding a small fixed fin and modifying the rudder. Similar alterations were made to the remaining

D.Is. Manufacture of the D.I ended early in 1917.

One or two D.Is were fitted with 200 h.p. Hiero engines, but the design was really incapable of supporting an engine of this power, and these may have been development machines for the Phönix D.I. This fighter, as its series numbers indicate, was a development of the Hansa-Brandenburg D.I. One Series 28 airframe (28.48) was fitted with unequal-span wings and a modified fuselage to test certain features of the Phönix design.

17 Austrian Aviatik D.I

The D.I single-seater by Aviatik was the first fighter of Austrian design to enter production during World War 1. It was the work of Dipl. Ing. Julius von Berg, and is often referred to as the Berg D.I or Berg Scout. It had its origins in the 30.14 aircraft which appeared early in 1916, although the true prototype was the 30.21 tested early in 1917. Production D.Is differed only in detail from this machine. Initial contracts were placed with six manufacturers: Aviatik (Series 38), Lloyd (Series 348), W.K.F. (Series 84), M.A.G. (Series 92), Thöne und Fiala (Series 101) and Lohner (Series 115). Repeat orders were placed with Aviatik for Series 138, 238 and 338; with Lohner for Series 215 (not built) and 315; with W.K.F. for Series 184, 284 and 384; and with Thöne und Fiala for Series 201 (not built). Total D.I production amounted to approximately seven hundred, although as many as one thousand two hundred may have been ordered. Standard powerplant was the 200 or 210 h.p. Austro-Daimler, but early and late production batches were fitted with 185 and 225 h.p. engines of the same manufacture.

Pilots were not enthusiastic about the D.I when it entered service in autumn 1917, in spite of its excellent flying characteristics and a comfortable, roomy cockpit which gave a good view over and under the top wing. Their dislike was directed chiefly at the Austro-Daimler engine, which easily became overheated; in service the top panels, and occasionally some of the side panels, were left off to assist cooling. The D.I's armament, which originally consisted of a single 8 mm. Schwarzlose machine-gun mounted over the top wing to fire upward over the propeller, was, by the time the type entered service, replaced by twin Schwarzlose guns, one on each side of the cylinder block; the precise position varied on different batches, frequently being installed with their breeches beyond the reach of the pilot, who was thus unable to clear the gun in the event of a stoppage. A satisfactory location was not achieved until the latter part of the D.I's service. The D.I was used widely until the Armistice by Austro-Hungarian units on the Balkan, Italian and Russian Fronts – particularly as protective cover for the *Fliegerkompagnien*'s 2-seaters, and rather less widely with the *Jagdkompagnien*, who in general preferred the German Albatros D.III; by mid-1918 only a few *Jagdkompagnien* were still equipped with Aviatik D.Is.

Developments included a prototype Dr.I triplane (30.24) completed in 1917, and the high-altitude D.III with a 230 h.p. Hiero engine, whose prototype (30.30) appeared in 1918. The only other production version was the D.II, generally similar to the D.I except for a cantilever lower wing; production of two Series (39 and 339) began late in 1918, but the D.II was too late for operational service.

18 Halberstadt D.I to D.V

The Halberstadt fighters came after the Fokker E.III had lost its supremacy and before the biplane fighters had fully regained it. Their performance was inferior to the Albatros D.I and D.II, but distinctly better than the indifferent early Fokker D types, and they were probably respected more by their Allied opponents than by their own pilots, who were dubious of the Halberstadts' slender lines and frail-looking tail unit. Such fears were quite unjustified, for the Halberstadt scouts were extremely strong machines that could withstand long, steep dives and tight manoeuvres better than most.

The D.I. was designed late in 1915, appearing in the following February. In its original form it had unstaggered wings and a 100 h.p. Mercedes D.I engine with side radiators; a single Spandau gun was offset to starboard in front of the cockpit. View from the cockpit was quite good; there was only a small gap between top wing and fuselage, and a semi-hexagonal cut-out in the trailing edge. The D.I was further modified into the D.Ia (120 h.p. Argus As.II in a cleaner cowling and a wing-mounted radiator). In this form, but with the Mercedes D.II, it entered production as the Halberstadt D.II, being built by Aviatik and Hannover in small numbers as well as by the parent company. It was followed by the Argus-powered D.III, which had larger, horn-balanced ailerons, vertical cabane struts and a semi-circular wing cut-out. The D.IV was generally similar except in having a 150 h.p. Benz Bz.III. Final variant was the D.V, which appeared early in 1917. This reverted to the Argus engine, but was considerably better streamlined, had simplified wing bracing and a neatly spinnered propeller. Provision existed to install a second gun in the D.IV and D.V, but as the Halberstadts' performance was already inferior to the Albatros fighters, it is unlikely that advantage was taken of this facility.

When it entered service in summer 1916, the D.II was issued in small numbers as an escort for 2-seat reconnaissance aircraft, but from early autumn it joined with the Albatroses in forming the composite equipment of several of the newly formed *Jagdstaffeln*. Peak employment was in January 1917, when a hundred D.II/IIIs were in front-line service in France, but after that winter they started to give way to the later Albatros variants. They were used for a few months longer in Macedonia and Palestine; a few D.IVs were supplied to Turkey.

19 Pfalz D.III

The Pfalz Flugzeug-Werke did not produce a biplane fighter of its own design until Rudolfo Gehringer's D.III appeared in the spring of 1917. It clearly owed much to the Roland fighters that Pfalz had been building under licence, but was slimmer, neater and even more shark-like than the Roland 'fish'. The Pfalz D.III was extremely well built, having a semi-monocoque ply fuselage, and the wings were of unequal chord to give a better downward view; Pfalz avoided the structural trap of similar designs by employing a two-spar lower wing. The fuselage–upper-wing gap was kept to a minimum to afford a good all-round view from the cockpit.

The prototype D.III was tested in June 1917 and went quickly into production with few modifications. Its twin Spandau guns were completely buried, except for their muzzles, in the front fuselage. The D.IIIa, which followed it into production, had a Mercedes engine offering upward of 175 h.p., and its guns mounted more conventionally on top of the fuselage, where they were easier to aim and to service. The wingtip shape on later D.IIIs and D.IIIas was altered to a more rounded form.

The D.III began to enter service in August 1917, being supplied first to Jastas in Bavaria. By 31 December 1917 two hundred and seventy-six D.IIIs and one hundred and fourteen D.IIIas were at the Front. The D.IIIs dwindled thereafter, while D.IIIa numbers rose in proportion. The D.IIIa reached its peak in April 1918 when four hundred and thirty-three were at the Front. Forty-six Jastas are known to have had some D.III/IIIas on strength, but the type only fully equipped about a dozen of these. The Pfalz fighters' reputation seems to have suffered in comparison with other late-war German fighters. Certainly they were not as fast as the Albatros D.Va, nor had they the altitude performance of the Fokker D.VII; nevertheless a prejudice against them seems to have existed among many German pilots, some of whose allegations – e.g. of structural weakness and a lack of manoeuvrability – are difficult to justify. The Pfalz was certainly not weakly constructed – indeed, it could be dived harder and faster than the Albatros, a factor that led to its extensive use on 'balloon-busting' activities. It was also an excellent gun platform and capable of absorbing a great deal of battle damage. The numbers in service, especially in the early spring of 1918, suggest that it played a larger part in retrieving German air superiority than it is generally given credit for. No production total can be quoted with certainty, but it is possible that as many as one thousand were built. The D.IIIa was gradually replaced by the Albatros D.Va and Fokker D.VII from spring 1918, but one hundred and sixty-six were still in service at the end of August.

20 L.F.G. (Roland) D.I to D.III

The early Roland fighters were designed by Tantzen as progressive single-seat developments of the 1915 C.II. The tubby, fish-like appearance of the C.II had earned it the nickname *Walfisch* (Whale), and the more slender lines of the D.I prototype which was flown in July 1916 inevitably led to it being named *Haifisch* (Shark). The prototype was powered by a 160 h.p. Mercedes D.III, retaining similar hemispherical spinner and side radiators to the C.II. Among differences from the C.II were unstaggered wings and a more angular tail assembly. A small window/escape hatch in the side of the nose was omitted on production D.Is. These were built from late 1916 by the parent company and Pfalz, with only minor changes from the prototype. Standard armament was a single forward-firing Spandau gun. In October 1916 the D.II was flown for the first time, this having a pylon-type cabane for the upper wing in an attempt to improve the view downward past the nose; other modifications having the same object included a wing-mounted radiator, cut-down cockpit sides and a downward-curving engine exhaust. A slightly longer and lighter variant with shorter-span wings and a 180 h.p. Argus As.III was designated D.IIa, and both these types entered service in the early months of 1917. Their standard armament consisted of twin Spandaus.

The operational career of these Roland fighters was undistinguished: the various changes had done little to improve the cockpit view, and they were still tricky to land. They were heavy on the controls and their overall performance was inferior to contemporary Albatros single-seaters. Hence they were generally relegated to fairly quiet sections of the Western Front, to Russia and to Macedonia.

The last production version was the D.III, powered by the As.III engine, which introduced a strutted cabane giving a small gap between fuselage and top wing, a reduced-chord lower wing and a longer vertical fin. One hundred and fifty D.IIIs were ordered, but only some twenty-five were delivered to front-line units; the remainder were used as advanced trainers. A development was the sole D.V, completed in 1917 with a D.III wing cellule and a 160 h.p. Mercedes in a slimmer fuselage. A twin-float development of the D.II, flown on 29 June 1917, also had a Mercedes D.III and was designated WD. Two C type machines appeared in 1917, the C.V and C.VIII. The C.V was based on the D.II, while the C.VIII apparently combined some features of the C.III and D.II and was powered by either a 260 h.p. Mercedes D.IVa or a 245 h.p. Maybach Mb.IV. None of these types achieved production status.

21 L.F.G. (Roland) D.VI

The Roland D.VI was one of several excellent German fighters produced in the last year of the war whose careers were eclipsed at least partially by the omnipresent Fokker D.VII. During the summer of 1917 L.F.G. produced a triplane designated D.IV, designed by Dipl. Ing. Tantzen. This did not enter production but was noteworthy as the first application to aircraft construction of the *Klinkerrumpf* method of fuselage building. The same method was used in the prototype D.VI which appeared late in 1917. This was powered by a 160 h.p. Mercedes D.III engine and had a small 'keel' on the underside of the fuselage to which the lower wing was attached. A pair of 7·92 mm. synchronised Spandau guns were mounted in front of the cockpit.

The D.VI entered production in two forms. The D.VIa was powered in similar fashion to the prototype, but as Mercedes engines were in short supply, the Benz Bz.IIIa, nominally rated at 150 h.p., was installed in the D.VIb. On later D.VIbs a high-compression version of this engine delivered 200 h.p. Both models were evaluated in the fighter competition at Adlershof in January/February 1918 when, like everything else, they were overshadowed by the Fokker D.VII. However, as a precaution against possible failure in the delivery of sufficient Fokkers, limited numbers of the Roland fighters were ordered.

As things turned out, there were no delivery delays with the Fokker fighters, and consequently the Roland D.VI saw little operational service. It entered use in the late spring and early summer of 1918, and in some respects was superior to the Fokker. The cockpit was roomy and comfortable, affording an excellent view in most directions, and the controls were said to be easier to operate than those of the D.VII. It had good short take-off character-

istics, an excellent rate of climb and at an altitude of 15,000 ft. (4,570 m.), which it could reach in 24 minutes, its speed was still in the region of 100 m.p.h. (161 km/hr.). Main disadvantages were its tricky landing characteristics (despite a low landing speed) and the tendency of the D.VIb's Benz engine to overheat. The German Navy also used the D.VIa and D.VIb to defend its seaplane bases along the northern European coastline. After the Armistice thirteen aircraft of this type were taken to the United States for evaluation.

22   Albatros D.I and D.II

Thanks largely to the D.H.2 and the Nieuport 11, the Allies had the measure of the Fokker monoplanes by the late spring of 1916, and Germany clearly needed a new fighter if she was to regain the air supremacy she had enjoyed during the previous winter. Some interim biplane fighters had appeared, with a forward-firing two-gun armament, but in general the weight of the extra gun and its ammunition caused a falling-off in performance. Clearly, more power was needed as well as more guns, and at the Albatros Werke the team under Dipl. Ing. Robert Thelen evolved a prototype known as the D.I which appeared in August 1916. This was armed with twin 7·92 mm. Spandau guns and was powered by a 160 h.p. Mercedes D.III.

The Albatros D.I was the first German fighter to carry a two-gun armament without suffering a corresponding loss of performance, and it quickly entered production, virtually unchanged from the prototype except for the fitting of horn-balanced elevators. It was less manoeuvrable than the Fokker monoplanes, but this factor was more than outweighed by its greater speed, climb and firepower. The appearance of the Albatros D.I coincided with the reorganisation of the German Air Service into *Jagdstaffeln*, and the first operations by D.I-equipped *Jastas* took place in September 1916. In December there were fifty D.Is in service at the Front, but by then they had already been replaced in production by the D.II, which had entered service in October. The D.I's chief limitation had been the rather poor forward view from the cockpit, and the D.II remedied this by having a reduced gap between the fuselage and upper wing and splayed-out 'N' pattern cabane struts. Further improvement was gained by replacing the D.I's side radiators with a flush-mounted wing radiator. By January 1917, their peak period of service, two hundred and fourteen D.IIs were at the Front, where their performance and firepower helped greatly to swing the balance of air superiority back in Germany's favour. The D.II was superseded by the later and even better D.III from January 1917, and by May the January figure of D.IIs at the Front had been exactly halved; by November the total of both D.Is and D.IIs at the Front had dwindled to twenty. German production of the D.II was shared by L.V.G., and a further twenty D.IIs were built for the Austro-Hungarian Air Service by Oeffag as the Series 53 with 185 h.p. Austro-Daimler engines.

After the end of the war, in order to circumvent the terms of the Armistice, all Albatros types were redesignated, the D.I becoming known as the L.15 and the D.II as the L.17.

23 Albatros D.III

The first of the Albatros 'V-strutters', the D.III was the best and most effective of all the Albatros fighters produced during World War 1. It resulted from an *Idflieg* request during 1916 for German designers to incorporate in their fighters some of the features that had made the Allied Nieuport scouts so successful on the Western Front. At the Albatros Werke, Dipl. Ing. Thelen decided to retain the basic fuselage of his D.II, with a high-compression version of the Mercedes D.III to give a better altitude performance, and to design an entirely new wing cellule. Following Nieuport practice, though less drastically, he made the lower wings much narrower in chord than the upper pair. The result was an aircraft with an even better speed and climb rate than the Albatros D.II, and when it joined the earlier Albatros fighters in service at the beginning of 1917 it quickly began to establish its superiority.

The first *Jastas* to receive the D.III included No. 11 in January 1917, and by that spring all 37 *Jastas* at the Front were fully or partly equipped with Albatros fighters of one kind or another. The D.III remained in service throughout the year, reaching its peak of service in November when four hundred and forty-six were at the Front. During this period it formed the major equipment of the *Jastas*, and was one of the chief agents of destruction in what the Allies came to know as 'Bloody April'. From July the D.III began to be joined in service by the D.V and D.Va, although D.III production did not come to an end until early the following year. In addition to their service on the Western Front, Albatros D.IIIs also operated with the German air service in Palestine and Macedonia, and three Series (53.21, 153 and 253) were built by Oeffag for the Austro-Hungarian air arm, powered respectively by 185, 200 and 225 h.p. Austro-Daimler engines.

Modifications introduced during the production life of the D.III included slightly offsetting the wing radiator to starboard – where, if punctured during combat, the scalding water would not fly into the pilot's face – and the fitting of a more rounded rudder, similar to that later used on the D.V; D.IIIs in Palestine were later fitted with twin radiators. During the latter part of 1917 the Albatros D.III was gradually outclassed by later Allied fighters, first by the Sopwith triplane and Spad VII and later by the Camel and S.E.5a.

Some German- and some Austrian-built D.IIIs were supplied to the Polish Air Force in 1919. The post-war designation of the Albatros D.III was L.20.

24 Albatros D.V and D.Va

The Albatros D.V was produced in an attempt, not entirely successful, to maintain the edge of superiority gained in 1917 by the excellent D.III, in the face of later Allied types such as the S.E.5a and Sopwith Camel. An interim model, the D.IV, had appeared in 1917, marking a return to the equal-chord wings of the D.II and powered by a fully enclosed geared Mercedes engine. Owing to troubles with this engine the D.IV was not developed, but its fuselage design was retained in the D.V, which resumed the more graceful and more efficient wing form of the D.III. The D.V's fuselage was of oval section (compared with the flat-sided D.III), and the high-compression Mercedes D.IIIa was installed with rather fewer pretensions to careful cowling in order to simplify access and maintenance. The D.V retained the same tailplane as the D.III, but introduced an integral fixed fin, a raked-back underfin and (except for the prototype) a more rounded rudder. Fuselage construction was lighter but stronger than that of the earlier Albatros fighters, although the gross weight of the D.Va was slightly increased over that of the D.V by virtue of additional strengthening. The D.V also differed from the other Albatros fighters in the arrangement of its aileron control wires, and this marked the only visible point of distinction between the D.V and D.Va.

Unfortunately, although flying qualities remained good, the D.V and D.Va were no great improvement over the D.III, and achieved their success as much by sheer weight of numbers as by their performance. First D.Vs were delivered to *Jastas* in mid-1917, D.Vas following from late autumn, both versions serving alongside their earlier stablemates. They reached their peak of service in November 1917 and March 1918 respectively, and were the most widely used of all Albatros fighters. Exact production figures are not known, but a minimum of one thousand five hundred and twelve D.V/Vas are known to have served with Western Front units, and this takes no account of aircraft with home establishments or those used in Italy and Palestine. Production was shared by the Ostdeutsche Albatros Werke.

Despite limitations on diving manoeuvres, imposed after a series of crashes caused by failure of the single-spar lower wings (also a weakness of the D.III), D.V/Vas remained in service until the Armistice. In the post-war redesignation of Albatros types the D.V/Va became known as the L.24.

25 Royal Aircraft Factory S.E.5 and S.E.5a

In summer 1916 two fighters were designed around the 150 h.p. Hispano-Suiza, the S.E.5 and the F.E.10. The latter was not adopted, but its fin and rudder shape was transferred to the S.E.5, the first of whose three prototypes (A4561) flew on 22 November 1916. This had a 27 ft. 11 in. (8·51 m.) wing span and was one of the first aircraft to use the Constantinesco syn-

chronising gear for its forward-firing Vickers gun. The S.E.5 was faster and stronger than the French Spads and Nieuports, although less manoeuvrable than the latter, and had excellent altitude performance, firepower and view from the cockpit. The first twenty-four S.E.5s had semi-enclosed cockpits, the Vickers gun offset to port and a drum-fed Lewis on a Foster mounting above the centre-section. The next batch were built with a reduced wing span of 26 ft. 7½ in. (8·12 m.).

The first S.E.5s were delivered to No. 56 Squadron R.F.C. in March 1917. As soon as they arrived in France their large windscreens were replaced by smaller ones before the squadron undertook its first operational sortie on 22 April. Fifty-nine S.E.5s were built by the Factory, all with Hispano-Suiza 8 A engines; Nos. 24, 60 and 85 Squadrons also received some S.E.5s, which remained in service until the end of the year.

Meanwhile A4563, the third S.E.5, had become, in effect, the prototype S.E.5a, with a 200 h.p. Hispano-Suiza and S.E.5 short-span wings. The S.E.5a went to Nos. 56, 40 and 60 Squadrons, from June 1917, and by the end of the year had been delivered to 24, 41, 68 and 84 Squadrons. Deliveries would have been more numerous but for trouble with the reduction gear of the bigger Hispano-Suiza and an acute supply shortage of these power-plants. Until French-built units became available early in 1918, British-built equivalents or alternatives were improvised, the best being the redesigned direct-drive version built by Wolseley as the Viper, which became the S.E.5a's standard powerplant and gave it its characteristic 'square-jawed' look. Engine difficulties did not prevent the S.E.5a from acquiring a fine reputation for its flying qualities, physical strength and performance, and it remained in service until the end of the war, sharing with the Camel the chief credit for regaining Allied air superiority in 1918. Some were fitted with under-fuselage racks for four 25 lb. Cooper bombs. The S.E.5a was also used in the Middle East and by a few Home Defence units in 1918. It was less successful as a night fighter, being difficult to land at night; moreover, its liquid-cooled engine took longer to warm up than the rotaries of other Home Defence fighters.

At the end of the war approximately two thousand seven hundred S.E.5/5as were on R.A.F. charge, and the type had served with twenty-four British, two U.S. and one Australian squadrons. Serial allocations had been made for nearly five and a half thousand S.E.5as; at least two hundred of these were cancelled at the Armistice, and not all of the others were delivered. In the United States Curtiss assembled fifty-six from British components, and built one all-American S.E.5a, which was flown on 20 August 1918. This was the first and only example completed of a contract for one thousand American-built S.E.5as. The S.E.5b, a cleaned-up sesquiplane conversion from an S.E.5a airframe, did not become a production model.

After the war the S.E.5a went out of R.A.F. service, but fifty were supplied to Australia, at least a dozen to Canada and others to South Africa, Poland and the United States. Fifty ex-R.A.F. machines came on to the British civil register, where in post-war days the S.E.5a became known chiefly for its pioneer work in the art of skywriting.

26 Pfalz D.XII

In the early months of 1918 Pfalz produced a prototype, believed to have been the D.XI, with a 180 h.p. Mercedes D.IIIa, a similar fuselage to the Pfalz D.III and wings resembling those of the Fokker D.VII. This did not enter production, and it seems reasonable to infer that the all-conquering Fokker had a marked influence on the Pfalz design team, for its successor, the D.XII, had contours even more like the Platz fighter. However, despite this strong external likeness, the constructional methods of the Fokker D.VII and Pfalz D.XII were quite different. The D.XII was a sound design, and a strong one, but by the latter part of 1918 German ground crews had become accustomed to the cantilever Fokkers and other types with little or no external bracing, and resented the additional work involved in rigging the much-braced Pfalz fighter.

Two prototypes, one with a Mercedes D.IIIa and the other with a 185 h.p. B.M.W. IIIa, were evaluated at Adlershof in May/June

1918. The Mercedes version was chosen for production, to augment supplies of Fokker D.VIIs. There is a popular belief that the Pfalz company, which enjoyed the support of the Bavarian government, may have used bribery to secure these contracts. Pfalz D.XIIs entered service in September 1918, being delivered during the remaining months of the war to ten *Jagdstaffeln*, including four Bavarian *Jastas* of JG IV. German units had been conditioned by extensive publicity for the Fokker D.VII into believing that anything else must be inferior, and the Pfalz machines were not given a warm welcome. Nevertheless, once pilots had become acquainted with them they found them fast, manoeuvrable aircraft that could cope adequately with Allied S.E.5as and Camels. Their climb was poor – they took twice as long as the Fokker to reach 5,000 m. (16,404 ft.) – but their stronger construction enabled them to be dived harder. They were armed with twin forward-firing Spandau guns. Like other good German fighters that appeared in 1918, their reputation was dwarfed by the exploits of the far more numerous Fokkers; had the war continued a little longer the Pfalz D.XII would probably have made a greater impact.

It is believed that about a hundred and seventy-five D.XIIs were surrendered at the Armistice, and for a year or two after the war some were used by civilian private owners in several European countries. Wartime variants included the D.XIV, with enlarged fin and 200 h.p. Benz Bz.IVü; and the D.XV, which was tested a week before the Armistice. Powered by a 185 h.p. B.M.W. IIIa, the D.XV had its lower wings separated from the fuselage and simplified interplane bracing. It is believed that it was earmarked for series production.

27 Fokker D.VII

The Fokker D.VII, widely claimed as the best German fighter of World War 1, was evolved to a specification issued late in 1917. Its true prototype was the Fokker V.11, designed by Reinhold Platz. With thirty other machines, six of them alternative Fokker designs, the V.11 was tested at Adlershof in January/February 1918. It proved superior to all other entrants by a wide margin, and with modifications made at the instigation of Rittmeister von Richthofen was immediately ordered for large-scale production: four hundred from Fokker, and substantial quantities from Albatros and O.A.W. The V.11 was somewhat unstable in a dive, and production D.VIIs therefore had a lengthened fuselage and a fixed vertical fin. There was an excellent view from the cockpit, and the D.VII was armed with twin 7.92 mm. Spandau guns, with 500 r.p.g., immediately in front of the pilot. It was easy to fly, but its main advance over earlier German fighters was its ability to maintain performance at high altitude. This was enhanced even further from late summer 1918 by the D.VIIF. powered by a 185 h.p. B.M.W,

IIIa. The D.VIIF was only fractionally faster than the D.VII, but had greater reserves of power above 5,000 m. (16,400 ft.), which height the D.VIIF could reach in 14 minutes, compared with the Mercedes D.VII's time of just over 38 minutes. Understandably, the D.VIIF was much sought after.

Von Richthofen's *Jagdgeschwader I* (later commanded by Hermann Goering) began to receive the first Fokker D.VIIs in April 1918. Customary practice was to allocate new fighters to *Jastas*, and to pilots within *Jastas*, in order of eminence, and several months elapsed before some lesser *Staffeln* were able to get D.VIIs. Nevertheless, by the time of the Armistice the Z.A.K. (Central Acceptance Commission) had accepted seven hundred and sixty D.VIIs, and the type had been delivered to forty-eight *Jastas*, although several units operated well below establishment. In all, Fokker built at least eight hundred and forty D.VIIs; seven hundred and eighty-five were ordered from Albatros, and nine hundred and seventy-five from the Ostdeutsche Albatros Werke. In Austro-Hungary the type was built by M.A.G. as the Series 93; a second Series (132) was ordered from the Austrian Aviatik company, but none of the latter were built.

Throughout summer and autumn 1918 the Fokker D.VII was treated with a respect afforded to no German fighter since the Fokker E.III three years earlier, and Article IV of the Armistice Agreement paid it a unique tribute by singling it out for specific mention among items of military equipment to be handed over to the Allies. This squashed Anthony Fokker's hopes of continuing in the aircraft manufacturing business in Germany after the war, and precipitated the now-famous smuggling episode in which he succeeded in getting four hundred engines and components of one hundred and twenty aircraft, most of them D.VIIs, out of Germany into Holland. The D.VII continued in production in Holland after the war, and remained in service, first with the Dutch Army Air Service and later in the Netherlands East Indies, until the late 1920s. Between 1919 and 1926 a number of ex-wartime D.VIIs were used, after conversion to 2-seaters, as trainers by the Belgian *Aviation Militaire*; twenty-seven were supplied to the Swiss *Fliegertruppe*.

28 Martinsyde G.100 and G.102 'Elephant'

Designed by A. A. Fletcher of Martinsyde Ltd. in mid-1915, the G.100 was the company's third biplane product. Conceived for long-range escort, it was large for a single-seater, and quickly earned the nickname 'Elephant'. The prototype (4735) was powered by a 120 h.p. Austro-Daimler in a rather bulky cowling, but a neater cowling and other improvements were introduced in the Beardmore-engined production version in late autumn 1915. These were delivered from early 1916 in twos and threes as escorts for squadrons of reconnaissance 2-seaters. These included

Nos. 18, 20, 21 and 23 Squadrons in France; Nos. 14, 67 and 142 in Palestine; and Nos. 30, 63 and 72 in Mesopotamia. The only R.F.C. squadron to be equipped solely with Elephants was No. 27, which arrived in France with them on 1 March 1916. The Elephant's main armament consisted of a Lewis gun over the top wing, firing at an angle over the propeller. A second Lewis could be mounted on a bracket behind the pilot's left shoulder, which, if he were something of a gymnast, he could operate to defend himself from the rear. The dubious value of this second gun, and its absence from most surviving photographs of the Elephant, suggest that it was usually omitted. In any event, the Elephant was too heavy and unresponsive, and the pilot's view too poor, for aerial fighting. On the other hand, its excellent stability and the good lifting properties of its broad wings made it eminently suitable for bombing and ground attack, and it was in the latter role that the Elephant achieved its greatest success. The G.100 could carry one 230 lb. or two 112 lb. bombs; maximum load of the later G.102, most of which had a 160 h.p. Beardmore engine, was increased to 260 lb., with an endurance of $4\frac{1}{2}$ hours.

The only visible difference between the G.100 and G.102 were the three stub exhausts of the latter (when the 160 h.p. engine was fitted) in place of the single manifold of the G.100. One hundred G.100s and one hundred and seventy G.102s were built, serving with the operational units already listed and with six training units in the United Kingdom. The Elephants of 27 Squadron remained in service until replaced by D.H.4s in November 1917, and those of No. 72 Squadron in Mesopotamia until as late as October 1918. Two aircraft from one Middle Eastern squadron operated against the Bolsheviks from Baku on the Caspian Sea. Experimental Elephants included 7298, used as trials aircraft for the wing-mounted Lewis gun, and A6299, which was used to evaluate an Eeman triple-gun mounting.

29   Martinsyde F.4 Buzzard

The Buzzard was evolved from the R.G. biplane, flown in February 1917. It first assumed its definitive form with the single-seat F.3, designed by G. H. Handasyde, which made its maiden flight in November 1917 powered by an experimental 285 h.p. Falcon engine. This was later replaced by a standard 275 h.p. Falcon III, and plans were made for quantity production; however, because of prior claim to the Falcon engine by the Bristol F.2B only six F.3s were ordered. Four were allocated to R.F.C. Home Defence units in 1918. An alternative version powered by the 300 h.p. Hispano-Suiza was evolved under the designation F.4. Apart from a repositioning of the cockpit further aft, the F.4 was essentially similar to the F.3 and was one of the fastest fighters of its day. Armament consisted of two synchronised Vickers machine-guns enclosed within the upper engine decking. Following its official trials in June 1918, the Buzzard, as the F.4 was then known, entered large-scale production for the R.A.F. By 31 October 1918 fifty-two were on R.A.F. charge, but none had become operational. Production continued for a while after the Armistice, the eventual number built being more than three hundred and seventy, all by the parent company. Cancelled contracts included five hundred from Boulton & Paul, two hundred from Hooper & Co. and three hundred from the Standard Motor Co. Plans to produce a further one thousand five hundred in the United States were also cancelled at the war's end.

The Buzzards built included two or three Mk. Ias intended as escort fighters for the Independent Force, but this version was not pursued. With the selection of the Sopwith Snipe as the standard post-war R.A.F. fighter, the Buzzard's service career was virtually at an end, although two served with the Communication Wing acting as couriers between London and Paris during the 1919 Peace Conference. The type also participated in the R.A.F. pageants of 1920 and 1922.

Before the liquidation of the Martinsyde company in 1921, a number of experimental and minor variants had appeared, including three F.4a and two F.6 2-seat civil tourers. A number of surplus Buzzards were purchased for resale by the Aircraft Disposals Co. between 1921 and 1930, some being re-engined with Armstrong Siddeley Jaguar radials under the designation A.D.C.1. Buzzards were sold to several foreign air forces, including those of Finland, the Irish Republic, Latvia, Portugal and Spain, and one was evaluated in Japan.

30 **Spad VII**

In 1915, foreseeing that the rotary engine had nearly reached the limit of its development, Marc Birkigt, Swiss-born chief designer of Hispano-Suiza, evolved a new water-cooled V-8 stationary engine promising an initial 150 h.p. It was around an engine of this type that Louis Bechereau produced in 1915 a tractor biplane known as the Spad V, forerunner of a strain of fighters that was to become famous in the final years of the war.

From the Type V, Bechereau developed the Spad VII, whose prototype flew at Villacoublay in April 1916 powered by a 140 h.p. Hispano-Suiza; it was armed with a forward-firing Vickers gun, offset slightly to starboard, whose synchronising gear was also designed by Birkigt. The new fighter immediately caught the fancy of the French authorities, who ordered two hundred and sixty-eight Spad VIIs. Delivery began on 2 September 1916, and ultimately five thousand six hundred Spad VIIs were built in France by eight manufacturers. Early aircraft had the 150 h.p. Hispano-Suiza 8 Aa, later models being given increased wing span and rudder area as the 180 h.p. and 200 h.p. models became available. One hundred Spad VIIs were built by the British Blériot and Spad Co., and a further one hundred and venty by Mann, Egerton. These ontracts were for the R.F.C. and .N.A.S. respectively but the .N.A.S. surrendered its Spad VIIs a return for the Sopwith triplanes aen on order for the R.F.C.

Although less manoeuvrable than ae Nieuports, the Spad VII was a rong, stable gun platform, with a rst-rate turn of speed and an xcellent climb to 12,000 ft. (3,660 a.). It filled a dire need when the ritish air forces in particular were quipped with ageing and vulner-ble pusher types. On the Western ront it served with numerous cadrilles de chasse, including the amous SPA.3 (Les Cigognes). From)ctober 1916 it equipped Nos. 19 nd 23 Squadrons R.F.C., and fteen were supplied to Escadrilles 5 nd 10 of the Belgian Aviation Ailitaire. Another nineteen, some tted in the field with a wing-aounted Lewis gun in addition to ae Vickers, were supplied to three R.F.C. squadrons in Mesopotamia, nd others went to training units in ae United Kingdom. Two hundred nd fourteen Spad VIIs were applied to Italy, where they quipped five squadriglie including ae celebrated 91a commanded by 'rancesco Baracca; a number were elivered to Russia, where they ometimes carried Le Prieur rockets a addition to their gun arma-aent. French squadrons began to e-equip with Spad XIIIs during aid-1917, and in December one undred and eighty-nine Spad VIIs vere bought by the United States, vhich allocated a proportion of them o seven squadrons of the A.E.F. in

Europe and sent the remainder home to serve as trainers.

After the war about a hundred Spad VIIs, many of them rebuilds, were supplied to the *Ecole Blériot* at Buc, and many others were sold to air forces all over the world.

31 Spad XIII

The Spad XIII was a development by Bechereau of his earlier Spad VII, with a 220 h.p. geared Hispano-Suiza 8 Ba and an armament of two forward-firing Vickers guns. The prototype (S392) first flew on 4 April 1917, and the Spad XIII went quickly into production, for it began to reach *escadrilles* of the *Aviation Militaire* at the end of May. It sub-sequently equipped over eighty *escadrilles*, and eight thousand four hundred and seventy-two Spad XIIIs were built, by the parent company and eight other French manufacturers. Between spring 1917 and the end of World War 1 it re-placed the Spad VII and Nieuport 28 in virtually all French fighter squadrons, and was flown by every leading French pilot of the period. The great French ace Georges Guynemer met his death while flying a Spad XIII.

The Spad XIII was also the prime equipment of sixteen squad-rons of the A.E.F. in France, which in February 1918 purchased eight hundred and ninety-three of these aircraft; *Escadrille* 10 of the Belgian *Aviation Militaire* flew Spad XIIIs and the R.F.C.'s No. 23 Squadron had some for a brief spell early in 1918. Spad XIIIs were also supplied to the Italian Air Force, where they are known to have served with the 77a and 91a *Squadriglie*, among others, but Italian pilots preferred the light and agile Hanriot HD.1 to the Spad XIII, and it was not widely used on the Italian Front.

The Spad XIII was a tricky aeroplane to handle at low speeds, but it was immensely strong and an excellent gun platform. Successive production batches had supercharged Hispano-Suiza 8 Be engines of 200 h.p. and finally the 8 BEc of 235 h.p. Wartime variants included the Spad XIICa.1, a contemporary of the prototype XIII; this had a 37 mm. Hotchkiss cannon in the engine Vee. Three hundred were built, but they were not a great success, the greater firepower being outweighed by the heavy recoil and the fact that the pilot was liable to be overcome by cordite fumes. A similar machine, on twin Tellier floats, was designated Spad XIV and handed over to the French Navy in November 1917. It had the creditable speed, for a seaplane, of 128 m.p.h. (206 km/hr.). In June 1918 the Spad XVII appeared, an enlarged twin-Vickers development of the XIII with a 300 h.p. Hispano-Suiza. Twenty Spad XVIIs were completed, being delivered to *Escadrille* SPA.3 (*Les Cigognes*), where they were flown by René Fonck and other leading French pilots. Six days before the Armistice the prototype was flown of the Spad XXIV, a fighter with a wheeled undercarriage designed for use aboard aircraft carriers.

After the Armistice, contracts were cancelled for about four thousand more French Spad XIII and six thousand due to be built b Curtiss in the United States. Fou hundred and thirty-five of th A.E.F.'s Spads were taken back t America, where they were eventu ally re-engined with direct-driv Wright-Hispano Es of 180 h.p redesignated Spad 13E and em ployed on training duties. Surplu French machines were sold to Bel gium (thirty-seven), Czechoslovakia Japan and Poland (forty). Th Italian Spads were retained o strength, and when the *Regia Aero nautica* was formed in 1923 Ital still had a hundred, mostly XIII in service. French Spad XIIIs wer withdrawn in 1923.

32 Austin-Ball A.F.B.1

At one time it was believed that th Austin-Ball fighter had bee designed by Captain Albert Bal V.C., D.S.O., M.C., and unt recently it was thought that th design originated early in 1916 when Ball wrote of 'a most wonderfu machine', the plans of which ha been sent to him in France. Howeve thanks to the researches of J. M Bruce, M.A., it has now been virtu ally established* that the design di not appear until late 1916 and tha Ball acted in a purely advisor capacity.

The A.F.B.1 was evidently initia ted as a private venture by th Austin Motor Co. Following a visi to Austin in December 1916, Bal

* See *War Planes of the First World Wa – Vol. One* (*Fighters*) by J. M. Bruc (Macdonald, 1965).

probably agreed to contribute practical advice, based on his experience as a fighter pilot. He was also instrumental in persuading Brigadier-General Sefton Brancker at the War Office to issue a contract for two prototypes.

Sadly, Ball never saw the A.F.B.1 fly, for he was killed in action on 7 May 1917 and the prototype was not flown at Martlesham until July. It performed well, its only weakness being a slight lack of lateral control. It was powered by a 200 h.p. Hispano-Suiza engine, and Ball's influence was apparent in the excellent field of view above and around the cockpit. Two 0·303 in. Lewis machine-guns were installed, one fixed centrally inside the fuselage behind the engine and firing through the hollow propeller shaft, the second on a Foster mounting over the upper wing, fixed to fire upward at an angle.

Because of the heavy S.E.5a production programme (in which Austin were involved) and its demand on the supply of Hispano-Suizas, the A.F.B.1 was not ordered into production. A second version was tested at Martlesham: unlike the first version, this had no sweepback, and interplane bracing was similar to that on the Spad VII, giving the single-bay A.F.B.1 the appearance of a 2-bay biplane. It is unclear whether this was the second of the two prototypes ordered, or merely a modification of the first.

33 Sopwith Dolphin

The first prototype Sopwith 5F.1 (as the Dolphin was originally known) was completed in May 1917, and after a short period of test flying by Harry Hawker was delivered to Martlesham for official trials. Apart from its backward-staggered wings, it departed from Herbert Smith's earlier designs in having a 200 h.p. Hispano-Suiza geared stationary engine. Twin forward-firing Vickers guns were enclosed under the engine decking. The second prototype had a smaller fin and a bigger, horn-balanced rudder, which improved controllability, but the aircraft was still criticised for its poor downward view. Despite this, the third prototype did away with the lower-wing cut-outs. This machine added two Lewis guns, mounted on the top-wing attachment frame to fire forward and upward, and with a few other minor changes (as seen on the fourth prototype) the Dolphin went into production.

Despite the demand for Hispano-Suizas for the S.E.5a, the first Dolphin contract, in June 1917, was for five hundred aircraft. A fortnight later two hundred more were ordered from the Darracq Motor Engineering Co., and a similar quantity from Hooper & Co. at about the same time. Deliveries began in the autumn of 1917. The first operational Dolphins were those of No. 19 Squadron, which replaced its Spads with them in January 1918. Three other Western Front squadrons – Nos. 23, 79 and 87 – also received Dolphins. At first they were not popular. With the engine 'in his lap' and fuel tanks immediately behind him, the pilot had a square steel-tube frame surrounding his neck, and his face was uncomfortably close to the butts of the overhead Lewis gun(s); understandably, he did not relish the prospect of his aircraft nosing over after a landing. Crash pylons were fitted experimentally, but were not introduced on any scale on aircraft in service. The twin Lewis guns were found to be more of a hindrance than a help, and often one or both were removed. Some 87 Squadron Dolphins had these guns remounted on the lower wings, outboard of the propeller arc. For ground attack the Dolphin could carry four 25 lb. Cooper bombs. Despite its faults, the Dolphin had a creditable operational record. One Home Defence squadron – No. 141 – also had Dolphins, but they were unsuccessful as night fighters; the Dolphins of No. 1 Squadron, Canadian Air Force, were not operational before the Armistice. Five were purchased by the American Expeditionary Force for evaluation.

At least one thousand five hundred and thirty-two Dolphins were built, most of them Mk.Is. The Mk.II was a proposed French-built version with a 300 h.p. Hispano-Suiza: a few were completed before the Armistice, but none are known to have become operational. Troubles with the Hispano-Suiza's reduction gear led to the Dolphin Mk.III, using a direct-drive version of the 200 h.p. engine. This underwent trials a few weeks before the Armistice. The Dolphin remained in service until mid-1919, after which most of those surviving

were scrapped, although some fought with Polish squadrons against the Russians in 1920.

34 Ansaldo A.1 Balilla (Hunter)

With a few exceptions (notably the Caproni bombers), the *Corpo Aeronautica Militare* was for the major part of World War 1 equipped with aircraft of French or British design. However, in the autumn of 1917 Ing. G. Brezzi of the Società Gio. Ansaldo brought out a prototype of the first native Italian single-seat fighter. Designated A.1, it was obviously influenced by the S.V. single-seater designed by Savoia and Verduzio which had flown in the previous March, although it was a much smaller aeroplane. The A.1 was a small, single-bay biplane with equal-chord, unstaggered wings and a hexagonal cut-out in the upper trailing edge. This afforded a good forward and upward view from the small cockpit, in front of which were twin 0·303 in. Vickers machine-guns under the top-decking, synchronised to fire forward between the propeller blades.

In November 1917, at the Turin airfield of the former Società Italiana Transaerea (which had been taken over as *Cantiere* 3 of the S.V.A. company earlier that year), the A.1 was put through its paces by three of Italy's most famous fighter pilots: Maggiore Francesco Baracca, Tenente-Colonnello Piccio and Capitano Ruffo di Calabria. The Italian airmen were enthusiastic about the Ansaldo fighter's high speed of nearly 140 m.p.h. (225·3 km/

hr.) and its generally good handling qualities. They were less enthusiastic about its manoeuvrability, which was considerably below that of the foreign fighters already serving with the Italian Air Force. Nevertheless, with a few minor modifications (which may have included a slight increase in wing span) the Ansaldo A.1 entered production on a limited basis and was named *Balilla*. One hundred and eight *Balillas* were built, but only a small proportion of these were issued to front-line squadrons. Most of the remainder were employed on Home Defence duties during the middle months of 1918.

After the war some Ansaldo A.1s were used as aerobatic display aircraft, and a small number were sold to Lithuania.

35 Nieuport-Delage 29

By far the finest fighter designed by Gustave Delage during 1914–18, the Nieuport-Delage 29 did not undergo its acceptance trials until late in 1918 and was thus too late to see wartime combat duty. Nevertheless, in the years immediately after the war it became the standard French fighter type, and as such makes an interesting comparison with the Sopwith Snipe (page 152). The NiD.29 departed from previous Delage practice in utilising a large stationary engine, the 300 h.p. Hispano-Suiza 8 Fb, instead of the now-outmoded rotary. The big Vee-type engine was enclosed in a neat cowling, with short stub exhausts, in a highly streamlined oval-section fuselage terminating in an elegantly curved tail assembly. The equal-span wings had only slight stagger, and wide-span ailerons almost the full width of each lower wing. Two distinctive egg-shaped Lamblin radiators were mounted between the undercarriage Vees. Two float-fitted Nieuport 29s were entered for the 1919 Schneider Trophy race, though they did not after all participate.

In its NiD.29C.1 production form the single-seat fighter was armed with twin synchronised forward-firing 0·303 in. Vickers guns almost completely encased by the engine cowling panels. It was produced in considerable numbers and equipped both fighter regiments of the re-formed *Aviation Militaire* after the Armistice, continuing to serve until 1929–30. The Nieuport 29's speed and manoeuvrability, and its excellent altitude performance, made it one of the most outstanding fighters of the 1920s. This is exemplified in its adoption by a number of foreign air forces. Licence versions were built by Nakajima (six hundred and eight for the Army Air Force in Japan), by SABCA (who built thirty for the Belgian *Aviation Militaire*) and by Macchi in Italy, who produced it in quantity for the *Regia Aeronautica*; about twenty were also supplied to the Royal Swedish *Flygvapnet*. The Japanese Nieuport 29s were still performing active combat duty during the Sino-Japanese war in 1931–32.

In addition to the height-record machine shown in the illustration, the Nieuport 29 featured in a number of speed events after the war. One modified racing aircraft reached 188 m.p.h. (302·5 km/hr.) in December 1919; this same aircraft won the 1920 Gordon Bennett Trophy and the *Coupe Deutsch* of 1922. A variant, the Nie.29G, was completed in 1918 for the *Marine Nationale*. This had a 180 h.p. Le Rhône rotary engine, but so far as is known remained a prototype only.

36 B.A.T. Bantam

The Bantam had its origins in a private venture, designated F.K.22 and known unofficially as the Bat, which flew in late autumn 1917 and was the first known design by Frederick Koolhoven after leaving Armstrong Whitworth earlier that year. The 120 h.p. A.B.C. Mosquito radial engine in this machine proved an utter failure, and alternative powerplants were chosen when six more F.K.22 prototypes (B9944–B9949) were ordered. Of the three completed by the end of 1917, B9944 and B9946 had a 170 h.p. A.B.C. Wasp I radial; B9945 was fitted with a 100 h.p. Gnome Monosoupape rotary, changed in early 1918 for a 110 h.p. Le Rhône.

At about this time the design was reviewed in relation to the Type I S.S. Fighter specification for the R.A.F., B9946 and the second trio of F.K.22s being redesignated F.K.23 and named Bantam Mk.I. The rotary-engined F.K.22 was retrospectively dubbed Bantam Mk.II. The four F.K.23s were completed to a variety of different configurations, all smaller than the original F.K.22. There is some doubt over which was the true prototype for the production

Mk.I: many authorities quote B9947, though B9949 was closer to the final form. A further nine Mk.Is (F1653–F1661) were built, the first four being delivered by April 1918. They were armed with twin synchronised Vickers machine-guns mounted at cockpit floor level and firing between the lower pair of engine cylinders on either side. The Bantam was fast and, in experienced hands, highly manoeuvrable, but exhibited dangerous spinning characteristics. One was taken to France in mid-1918, where it was test-flown at Villacoublay; another was evaluated in the United States. One Bantam I was fitted with a 200 h.p. Wasp II radial, with which it achieved 146 m.p.h. (235 km/hr.). Two other Wasp II-powered machines (J6579 and J6580) were ordered, but apparently not completed.

The mettlesome Wasp engine, whose sound was likened by one observer to 'thousands of empty wooden boxes falling on a stone floor', was still giving trouble, and its development was ultimately abandoned. By this time the war was over, the need for the Bantam no longer existed, and in any case the British Aerial Transport Co. had lost its separate identity. Seven Bantam Is found their way to the British civil register, two flying in the Fourth Aerial Derby on 21 June 1919, one with shortened lower wings. The final Bantam I (F1661/ G-EAYA) was taken to Holland by Koolhoven in 1924 where, as H-NACH, with a 200 h.p. Lynx engine and other modifications, it achieved 246 km/hr. (152·8 m.p.h.).

37 Sopwith Tabloid

A small, neat tractor biplane, the Tabloid was designed in 1913 as a racing aircraft with two side-by-side seats. Its square fuselage housed a neatly cowled 80 h.p. Gnome rotary engine, and had a small, balanced rudder at the rear. The wings were controlled by warping. Flown at Farnborough on 29 November 1913 by Harry Hawker, the Tabloid achieved a level speed of 92 m.p.h. (148 km/hr.) and climbed to 1,200 ft. (366 m.) in 1 minute. On 20 April 1914 a single-seat version flown by Howard Pixton won the 1914 Schneider race at an average 86·78 m.p.h. (139·66 km/hr.) – very nearly double the speed of the 1913 winner. The Schneider machine had a 100 h.p. Monosoupape engine, a small fixed fin, plain rudder and twin floats.

At about the same time the Tabloid entered military production. These aircraft retained the original 80 h.p. Gnome and wheel-and-skid landing gear, but were otherwise similar to the Schneider machine. When war broke out only a handful were in service with the R.F.C., but these were taken to France at the earliest opportunity. Major J. T. B. McCudden, V.C., in his book *Five Years in the Royal Flying Corps*, records the arrival of the first pair of R.F.C. Tabloids at St. Quentin on 27 August 1914 with the comment: 'they did not avail us much as fighting machines, in that they were not fitted in any way with firearms, but they could and did perform excellently from the scouting point of view'. This lack of armament was a serious handicap to most scouting aircraft in the early months of the war. Some Tabloids eventually mounted a rifle or Lewis gun on the fuselage or top wing to fire at an angle outside the propeller arc, and at least one Tabloid had steel deflector plates fitted to the propeller blades so that a Lewis gun strapped to the starboard side of the fuselage could fire between them as they turned. The R.N.A.S., which had the major share of the small number of Tabloids built, was quick to make more belligerent use of its machines: two aircaft, each carrying a small load of 20 lb. bombs, made successful attacks on the railway station at Cologne and the Zeppelin works at Dusseldorf on 7 October 1914. Overall production of the Tabloid, which came to an end in June 1915, is believed to have totalled about forty aircraft. Some R.N.A.S. Tabloids served in the Dardanelles and the Aegean, including two carried by H.M.S. *Ark Royal*.

38 Royal Aircraft Factory S.E.2

At the Royal Aircraft Factory in 1912 Geoffrey de Havilland designed the B.S.1, forerunner of all single-seat scouts, which had the remarkable speed for its day of 92 m.p.h. (148 km/hr.). It crashed in March 1913, but was rebuilt in modified form and redesignated S.E.2 (Scout Experimental No. 2). (The earlier S.E.1 was an entirely unrelated design of tail-first pusher configuration.)

In mid-1914 the S.E.2 underwent further modification, in which the original monocoque rear fuselage was replaced with a wood-and-fabric structure (a seemingly retrograde step), the engine cowling, landing gear skids and tail unit were revised, and a small pointed spinner was fitted to the propeller. In this form (in which it has since been referred to unofficially as the S.E.2a), it was re-flown on 3 October 1914, and later that month was taken to France to join No. 3 Squadron at Moyenneville. Its arrival was noted by Major J. T. B. McCudden, V.C., in his book *Five Years in the Royal Flying Corps*, with the observation that it was 'a little faster than the Bristols* with the same engine, but did not climb quite as well'. The S.E.2 remained at the Front until March 1915, but lacked the necessary armament to take full advantage of its undoubted fighter-like qualities. At first its pilot, Lt. Shekleton, had nothing but his Service revolver; later, a pair of rifles were fixed, one on each side of the fuselage, so as to fire at an angle outside the propeller arc. The question of an armed development of the S.E.2 was presumably not pursued because of production orders already in hand for the Bristol Scout.

In 1914 the basic conception of the S.E.2 was taken a stage further in the S.E.4, which was as advanced for 1914 as the B.S.1 had been in 1912. Flown for the first time in June 1914, the S.E.4 showed excellent flying qualities and later

---

* The Bristol Scout B.

achieved 135 m.p.h. (217 km/hr.) in level flight. This speed was an unofficial world record, although never claimed as such, and was matched by very few other aircraft in existence when the war ended four years later. The S.E.4 was wrecked in August 1914 when a section of the undercarriage collaped during a landing.

39 Royal Aircraft Factory B.E.8

Appearing late in 1912, as a development of the B.E.3 and B.E.4 of 1911, the B.E.8 was the only rotary-engined aircraft designed by the Royal Aircraft Factory to be built in quantity. It was an unarmed 2-seat biplane with a communal cockpit and warp-controlled wings; two prototypes were completed in 1912 and a third early in 1913. Powerplant was an 80 h.p. Gnome. In August 1913 the B.E.8 was ordered for the R.F.C., production aircraft having separated cockpits and a small fixed fin. Vickers built eleven, of fifteen ordered, and the first of these was delivered in April 1914. A further six were completed by the British & Colonial Aeroplane Co., and there are known serial allocations for at least six more B.E.8s.

The B.E.8s were issued in small numbers to various R.F.C. squadrons from May 1914, and some of these went to France in August. Their operational career was evidently haphazard and undistinguished, and by May 1915 there were only two operational B.E.8s in France. At one time or another Nos. 1, 3, 5, 6 and 7 Squadrons of the R.F.C. had B.E.8s on strength; the type was also used by the Central Flying School, from pre-war, and in July 1915 one B.E.8 was in service with No. 3 Flight R.N.A.S. Several were lost in accidents in France and many others were recalled for employment at training establishments in the United Kingdom. Deliveries began in March 1915 of the B.E.8a, which had shorter-span, B.E.2c-type wings with aileron control, a lower-set tailplane and (on some aircraft) a rounded fin. Powerplant remained the 80 h.p. Gnome, but several B.E.8s were given 80 h.p. Clergets early in 1916 and at least one aircraft was fitted experimentally with a 100 h.p. Monosoupape.

Thirty-eight B.E.8as were delivered to the R.F.C., although another five or more may have been completed. Twenty four of these were built by Vickers and the remainder by Coventry Ordnance Works. The B.E.8a was employed exclusively as a trainer.

40 & 41 **Avro 504**

In a production life spanning well over a decade more than ten thousand Avro 504s were built, and some were still in service at the outbreak of World War 2. Yet Sir Alliott Verdon-Roe, when he designed the aeroplane in 1913, thought he would be lucky to get an order for six; and indeed there was a time, in 1915, when it looked as if the Avro 504's development would be suspended in favour of the B.E.2c.

The prototype 504 flew at Brooklands in July 1913, bearing a close resemblance to the Avro 500, or Type E, already on order for the R.F.C. In November 1913, after modification, it underwent trials at the Royal Aircraft Factory, where it flew at 80·9 m.p.h. (130·2 km/hr.). In February 1914 it set an official British altitude record of 14,420 ft. (4,395 m.). Twelve Avro 504s were ordered by the War Office and one by the Admiralty. Eventually sixty-three were completed, a few of which served on reconnaissance with the R.F.C. in France in the early months of the war; one became the first British aircraft lost to enemy action, on 22 August 1914. The R.N.A.S. operated its 504s in more belligerent fashion, on several early bombing raids in which they usually carried four 16 lb. or 20 lb. bombs. The Avros' most celebrated raid was that made on 21 November 1914 against the Zeppelin sheds at Friedrichshafen. Naval 504s also undertook ground strafing, with a Lewis gun provided for the observer in the front cockpit.

First major production versions were the 504A and 504B, for the R.F.C. and R.N.A.S. respectively. The 504As had shorter-span ailerons, while Naval 504Bs retained standard ailerons and introduced a fixed vertical fin. A Scarff gun-ring could be mounted on a frame in the rear cockpit, but most 504Bs were used for training. A few were fitted with 80 h.p. Le Rhônes, but standard powerplant for both the 504A and 504B remained the 80 h.p. Gnome.

Early attempts to turn the 504 into an anti-Zeppelin fighter resulted in the 504C and 504D single-seaters, with covered-in front cockpits. Eighty 504Cs were built, some with an upward-firing Lewis; only six 504Ds were completed. One 504C was converted in 1916 into the experimental Avro 504F with a 75 h.p. Rolls-Royce Hawk; an order for thirty 504Fs was later rescinded.

The first major power increase came in the Avro 504E, a 2-seater for the R.N.A.S. with a 100 h.p. Monosoupape, considerably less wing stagger, a new fuel system and the rear cockpit positioned further aft. The Avro 504G was a naval conversion of the 504B for gunnery training, with a synchronised Vickers front gun and a Scarff ring in the rear cockpit. The 504H was a converted 504C, strengthened for trials with R. F. Carey's aircraft catapult.

By late 1916 the Avro 504 had been too far overtaken in performance to remain an effective combat aircraft. However, its first-class flying qualities made it ideal for training, and in this role the 504 made its greatest impact. First variant specifically for flying training was the 504J, which appeared in autumn 1916. This retained the characteristics of earlier R.F.C. machines and was powered by a 100 h.p. Monosoupape. The Avro 504J was an almost ideal *ab initio* trainer, and was the first aircraft to be chosen for this role when the R.F.C. began to put its flying training on a systematic footing. It was on an Avro 504J that Prince Albert (later King George VI) first learned to fly. It was ordered in substantial quantity, some 504A contracts being amended to specify Js, and new-production 504Js became available from early 1917.

The Avro 504J was not officially declared obsolete until 1921, but because of the variety of engines being fitted to the wartime trainers Avro developed the 504K, with an engine mounting that could be adapted to any of the available powerplants. Many Avro 504Ks were thus converted Js, or even As. The K model continued throughout the war and for many years after as a standard R.A.F. trainer and with many Commonwealth air forces. Meanwhile, early in 1918 it had been resurrected for another combat role, as an emergency anti-Zeppelin fighter. The 110 h.p. Le Rhône-engined 504K, selected for its 18,000 ft. (5,486 m.) ceiling, was converted to a single-seater by covering over the front cockpit and mounting a Lewis gun above the top wing. It equipped Six Home Defence squadrons during 1918, still serving with five of them at the Armistice. Final wartime model was the 504L, a converted K with a fixed fin, twin landing floats and a tail float. The 504M of 1919 was a 3-seat cabin tourer powered by a 110 h.p. Le Rhône or a 150 h.p. Bentley B.R.1: this had rather poorer flying qualities and was not a success.

Wartime production of 504s included three thousand six hundred and ninety-six by Avro and four thousand six hundred and forty-four by fifteen other British manufacturers. Five thousand four hundred and forty-six went to the R.F.C./R.A.F., two hundred and seventy-four of them to Home Defence units, nine to the Western Front and three hundred and ninety-two to the Middle East. The remainder were allocated to training units. Fifty-two were bought by the A.E.F. in July 1918; one hundred were to have been built in Canada, but only one or two were actually completed; several, powered by 100 h.p. Sunbeam Dyak engines, operated in Australia after the war. Avro 504s were built in Russia after the Revolution, called U-1 and powered by a copy of the Le Rhône. Developments included the Avro 519 2-seat fighter of 1916 (150 h.p. Sunbeam Nubian) and the Avro 521, a Clerget-engined fighter. These did not proceed beyond the prototype stage, an order for twenty-five Avro 521s being cancelled.

Many war-surplus Avro 504s found their way to the British civil register. They were used widely throughout the 1920s at flying schools, for joy-riding and aerial advertising. Many others went to military or civil owners abroad, including Belgium, Cuba, Guatemala, Norway and Sweden.

42 Bristol Scout

The Bristol Scout had most of the attributes necessary to make a good fighting machine: with a more effective armament it could have been a great one, at a time when such a weapon was needed urgently by the Allies. That it was not kept in production when more effective armament systems became available may have been due to the company's preoccupation by then with the Bristol F.2A and F.2B. The original design

by F. S. Barnwell was completed in February 1914 and achieved the excellent speed for its day of 95 m.p.h. (152·8 km/hr.).

By the outbreak of war on 4 August 1914 two further Scouts had been built, although neither had flown. These were immediately requisitioned by the War Office, given the military serials 633 and 648, and allocated to Nos. 3 and 5 Squadrons R.F.C. in France. In November 1914 the War Office ordered twelve generally similar Scout Cs for the R.F.C., and a month later twenty-four Cs were ordered for the R.N.A.S. Retrospectively, the original aircraft became known as the Scout A and the first two R.F.C. aircraft as Scout Bs. Deliveries of Scout Cs began in April and February 1915 respectively. Eventually, eighty-seven Scout Cs were delivered to the R.F.C. and seventy-four to the R.N.A.S. Twenty-two of the former and all of the latter were powered by 80 h.p. Gnomes and the remaining sixty-five R.F.C. Scouts by 80 h.p. Le Rhônes. At first these were mostly unarmed, although varied combinations of small arms were added by units in the field and some were later fitted with machine-guns. Captain L. G. Hawker of No. 6 Squadron R.F.C. won his V.C. on a Scout C when, on 25 July 1915, he shot down two German 2-seaters. Some R.N.A.S. Scouts carried Ranken darts for anti-Zeppelin missions or four small bombs under the fuselage.

Meanwhile, Barnwell had produced the Scout D, completed in

November 1915. An initial fifty Scout Ds were completed with C type wings and enlarged rudders; the remaining eighty Scout Ds for the R.F.C. were built to standard D pattern. The R.N.A.S. received eighty Scout Ds, sixty with 100 h.p. Gnome Monosoupapes and the remainder, for use as trainers, with 80 h.p. Gnomes. Provision existed on the Scout Ds for Vickers guns with Challenger synchronising gear, although most were issued in an unarmed state. In practice it seems that the R.N.A.S. preferred to use the non-synchronised overwing Lewis rather than the synchronised Vickers.

The Scout never became the sole equipment of any one squadron, but was issued in small numbers to almost every unit of the R.F.C., including nineteen squadrons on the Western Front, three in Palestine, two in Mesopotamia, one in Macedonia and one Home Defence squadron. Ten R.N.A.S. Home Defence units, one unit on the Western Front and two in the Aegean area were equipped with Scouts; the aircraft carrier H.M.S. *Vindex* carried two Scout Cs. One Scout figured in an interesting experiment when it was carried aloft on the upper wing of the prototype Porte Baby flying boat, a successful air separation being made on 17 May 1916. The object of this was to increase the Scout's anti-Zeppelin range, but the project was not developed further.

Some Scouts were still serving as fighters in the spring of 1917, but in general they had been almost completely withdrawn from front-line service by mid-1916, and transferred to training duties. One Scout was allocated to the Australian Central Flying School, and another was evaluated by the U.S. Army Engineering Division.

At the end of the war Bristol Scouts remaining in store were not considered suitable for restoration to flying standard; only one, a Scout D, came on to the British civil register, though this survived until 1930.

43 Nieuport 10 and 12

It is a pity that clearer records of the early Nieuport types have apparently not survived, for the sesquiplane 'V-strutters' of the Société des Etablissements Nieuport were among the most attractive and successful warplanes of 1914–18. Their basic design was the handiwork of Gustave Delage, who joined the Nieuport company in January 1914. His first design was the Nieuport 10, a tractor biplane with a body similar to the pre-war Nieuport monoplanes. A 2-seater, it appeared in two forms: the Nie. 10AV and Nie.10AR. The suffixes signified *avant* (in front) and *arrière* (behind), indicating the observer's position in relation to the pilot; the Nie.10AR may have served as prototype for the larger Nieuport 12.

Production Nie.10A.2s were issued to observation squadrons of the *Aviation Militaire* in the summer of 1915, but within a few months most of them were converted to single-seat Nie.10C.1s to undertake temporary fighting duties. The conversion was simple, consisting of covering in the front seat and mounting a Lewis machine-gun over the top wing to fire upward over the propeller. The reconnaissance Nie. 10A.2s carried a similarly mounted gun, operated by the observer, who had to stand up and put his head and shoulders through a small cut-out in the top wing. French-built Nieuport 10s were supplied to Britain and Belgium, and in 1916 some were built by Macchi for the Italian Air Force. Like the French machines, these were intended originally for reconnaissance, but were obliged to become stop-gap fighters.

The Nieuport 12 was a slightly enlarged version with a 110 h.p. or 130 h.p. Clerget 9 B rotary instead of the 80 h.p. Gnome or Le Rhône 9 C of the Nieuport 10. This type was also used by both British air services. Unfortunately, R.F.C. and R.N.A.S. serial allocations did not always specify an exact variant, records simply showing 'Nieuport' or 'Nieuport Scout'. Serials have been confirmed for one hundred and sixty-nine Nieuport 10/12s ordered by the R.N.A.S., which include fifty built by Beardmore Aviation, later machines having a small fixed vertical fin. Some of the sixty-three unclassified Nieuports whose serials are known may also have been Nieuport 10s or 12s. Twenty-one R.N.A.S. Nieuport 12s were transferred to the R.F.C., but only another ten serials can be confirmed for R.F.C. Nie.12s. There are a hundred and forty-five other known R.F.C. serials for Nieuport aircraft, and a few of these may

have been Nieuport 10s and/or 12s.

After the Nieuport 11 single-seat fighter entered service, the French, British and Italian 2-seaters were gradually withdrawn to training duties. The Le Rhône 9 C seems to have been standard for trainer derivatives of the Nieuport 12, which included the Nieuport 80E.2, 81D.2 (dual controls) and 83E.2 (communal cockpit). One hundred and forty-seven, one hundred and seventy-three and two hundred and forty-four respectively of these three variants were sold to the A.E.F. late in 1917.

44 Nieuport 11 and 16

The Nieuport 11 had its origins in a small, single-seat biplane, powered by an 80 h.p. Gnome engine, designed by Gustave Delage to compete in the 1914 Gordon Bennett race. The race was cancelled by the onset of World War 1, but the Nieuport 11 was quickly accepted for production as a fighter for the *Aviation Militaire*. Its diminutive size quickly earned it the nickname *Bébé* (Baby) when it entered service in the summer of 1915. A second early customer was the R.N.A.S.: six are known to have served with No. 3 Wing R.N.A.S., and since the type also served with No. 1 Wing, it seems reasonable to guess that at least a dozen of the 'Nieuport Scouts' for which R.N.A.S. serial numbers were allocated were of the Nieuport 11 type. From March 1916 they also served in France with the R.F.C., sharing with the D.H.2 and the F.E.2b the task of overcoming the Fokker monoplanes. There are no known R.F.C. serials for Nieuport 11s, although five numbers were allocated to 'Nieuport 13s'. These may have been Nieuport 11s, which were sometimes referred to as '13s' – a reference to their metric wing area, and not an official designation. Many other R.F.C. serials were allocated to unspecified 'Nieuport Scouts', and doubtless some of these were Nieuport 11s. Standard powerplants were the 80 h.p. Gnome and Le Rhône rotaries, and the Nie.11 was usually armed with a single Lewis gun over the top wing. In addition to service in France, the Nie.11 was also used in the Dardanelles by the R.N.A.S.; in Italy, Macchi built six hundred and forty-six Nie.11s, which were standard fighters in Italy and Albania until summer 1917. Others served in Belgium and Russia, and five were sold to the Netherlands, where a further twenty were later built under licence.

In 1916 a more powerful variant appeared: the Nieuport 16, powered by a 110 h.p. Le Rhône and mounting a synchronised Vickers gun for the pilot instead of the overwing Lewis. Some Nie.16s carried Le Prieur rockets on the interplane struts, with which they achieved some success in shooting down enemy observation balloons. It seems that the Nie.16 did not see service with the R.N.A.S.; it is known to have served with Nos. 29 and 60 Squadrons R.F.C., but the overall number in British service is not known. There are nine serial alloca-

tions for R.F.C. Nieuport 16s, though as explained earlier others may be 'hidden' in the large numbers of unidentified Nieuports.

During the critical period when the Fokker monoplane reigned supreme over the Western Front both the Nieuport 11 and 16 performed valiant service. They were flown by many celebrated French squadrons and pilots, including de Rose, Guynemer and Nungesser of *Escadrille* N.65. After the Nieuport 16 appeared, some Nieuport 11s were withdrawn for conversion to 2-seat trainers, and refitted with Clerget 7 Z engines.

45 Nieuport 17

The Nieuport 17 retained the 110 h.p. Le Rhône used in the Nieuport 16, differing chiefly from earlier Nieuports in having wings of increased span and area. Because of this it was often called the Nieuport '15' or '15-metre', which was the approximate area of the new wings. The Nieuport 11's single-spar lower wings had been liable to twist when the aircraft was dived or manoeuvred tightly, and a stronger spar was therefore fitted to the Nieuport 17.

In service the Nie.17 became one of the most successful and popular fighting aircraft of the entire war, both for its flying qualities and its fighting ability. In days when premier fighter pilots could virtually choose their own mounts, the inclusion of names like Ball, Bishop, Boyau, Guynemer and Nungesser among those who flew the little Nieuport is its own recommendation. It had a fine view from the cockpit, was a first-class dog-fighter and in the words of Commander C. R. Samson, R.N.A.S., climbed 'like a witch'. It also had a reputation for 'balloon-busting' with Le Prieur rockets. Early Nieuport 17s fought with a Lewis gun on a Foster mounting over the top centre-section, but a single synchronised Vickers replaced this on later machines. Individual essays were made with twin-gun installations, but these were found to impose an unacceptable performance penalty.

First French unit to receive the Nieuport 17 was *Escadrille* N.57 on 2 May 1916; other French *escadrilles* included N.3, N.38, N.55, N.65 and N.103. British Nieuport 17s joined their French comrades in service within weeks, eventually serving with Nos. 1, 2, 3, 6, 8, 9, 10 and 11 Squadrons R.N.A.S. and Nos. 1, 29, 32, 40 and 60 Squadrons R.F.C. on the Western Front. The type was also used by the R.F.C. in Macedonia. The number in British service is indeterminate: only eighty-nine known serial numbers (all for R.F.C. machines) apply specifically to Nieuport 17s, but this was clearly a fraction of the overall total. One authority quotes a figure of five hundred and twenty-seven Nieuport 11/17s in R.F.C./ R.N.A.S. service, most of which would have been 17s. One hundred and fifty Nieuport 17s were built in Italy by Macchi; it was built in and served in Russia; twenty were supplied to the Dutch Army Air Service in 1917, others to the Belgian *Aviation Militaire* and two to

Finland. Seventy-six were purchased by the A.E.F. as pursuit trainers. In August 1917 there were still three hundred and seventeen Nieuport 17s in front-line French service.

Late-production aircraft with 130 h.p. Clerget 9 B engines were designated Nieuport 17*bis*. The Nieuport 21 was a 2-seater trainer conversion with an 80 h.p. Le Rhône: one hundred and ninety-eight were sold to the United States in 1917–18. The Nieuport 23, built for French, British and American use, had improved streamlining and tail surfaces similar to those that appeared later on the Nieuport 28. Some Nieuport 23s were sold after the war to the Swiss *Fliegertruppe* and several single- and 2-seaters became sporting or privately owned aircraft in the days of peace. The success of the Nieuport fighters, and the Nieuport 17 in particular, was maintained even against the theoretically superior Albatros D.I and the early Halberstadt fighters, and it is no small tribute to the French machines that later German fighters were designed on instructions that they should incorporate many of the features that had made the Nieuports so outstanding.

46 Nieuport 24 and 27

First flown in 1916, the Nieuport 24 was a logical development of the Nieuport 17*bis* via the Nieuport 23 and was the first production Nieuport fighter in which a circular-section fuselage and a fixed vertical fin were introduced as standard. A parallel version, the Nie.24*bis*, however, retained the rudder-only configuration of the Nie.17; some aircraft also differed from standard in having rectangular wingtips. Standard armament comprised two forward-firing machine-guns mounted in front of the cockpit. The Nieuport 27 was generally similar except for revised armament and undercarriage details.

Although conceived as a fighter (Nie.24C.1), the Nieuport 24 would seem to have been used only for training duties (Nie.24E.1) by the *Aviation Militaire*. The only known operational Nieuport 24s were a batch of fifty Nie.24*bis* built for the R.N.A.S. by the British Nieuport and General Aircraft Co., although some may have been used in combat by the Belgian and Italian air forces. The R.F.C. had at least three Nieuport 27s; a small batch was supplied by France to Italy, where others were later built by Nieuport-Macchi. Largest known user of the two types was the A.E.F., which purchased one hundred and twenty-one Nie.24s and one hundred and forty Nie.24*bis* late in 1917 as pursuit trainers. The A.E.F. also ordered two hundred and eighty-seven Nie.27s at about the same time, but no more than one hundred and twenty of these may have been delivered.

The Nie.24 and Nie.27 represented the peak of development of the basic V-strutted sesquiplane layout but, by the time they appeared, French front-line fighter squadrons were already equipping or equipped with faster Spads. One Nie.24 was completed with a larger, two-spar lower wing and used as a development aircraft in the evolution of the Nieuport 28.

47 Nieuport 28

First of the 'new look' Nieuports, the Nie.28 was of much more conventional appearance than the earlier 'V-strutters'. Unfortunately its effectiveness as a fighter did not live up to the elegance of its design. The prototype, later serialled 4434, flew for the first time on 14 June 1917. A single 0·303 in. Vickers gun was mounted just below the centre-section struts on the port side. It was ordered into production as the Nie.28C.1 by the French government, although few, if any Nie.28s saw service with the *Aviation Militaire*. Changes made to production aircraft included revised tail surfaces, dihedral on the top wing, increased gap between the top wing and fuselage, and a second Vickers gun just left of centre on the top decking.

The Nieuport 28 might have drifted into obscurity, but it chanced to appear when no other fighter was readily available to pursuit squadrons of the A.E.F. early in 1918. Two hundred and ninety-seven Nie.28s were purchased by the United States and issued to the 27th, 94th, 95th and 147th Aero Squadrons in France. Delivery of these started in March, but the first combat patrols did not take place until the following month, due to delay in receiving their guns. Some aircraft had 0·30 in. Marlin guns instead of the Vickers weapons, and a few are believed to have carried out 'balloon-busting' duties using an 11 mm. Vickers gun in the upper position. Leading American Nieuport 28 pilots included her first 'ace', Lt. Douglas Campbell, and her highest-scoring fighter pilot, Capt. E. V. Rickenbacker. Raoul Lufbery and Quentin Roosevelt lost their lives while flying Nieuport 28s. Although it was light, manoeuvrable, and had a rapid acceleration, the Nie.28 had an unhappy tendency to shed its upper-wing fabric in any violent manoeuvre; but its most unfortunate feature was the thoroughly unreliable Gnome Monosoupape engine. Various machines were fitted experimentally with Clerget, Hispano-Suiza or Lorraine engines, but the wretched Gnome remained the standard unit. From July 1918 the A.E.F. began to replace its Nie.28s with Spad XIIIs, relegating the Nieuports to training duties.

Fifty or more surviving Nieuport 28s were taken back to the United States in 1919, twelve being transferred subsequently to the U.S. Navy for shipboard use. After a short post-war spell of training duty the Army scrapped or sold its remaining Nie.28s. A few found their way to civil owners, some having their wings cropped and being flown as racing aircraft during the early 1920s. A number were also sold to the Royal Hellenic Army Air Service, and fourteen to the Swiss *Fliegertruppe*.

8 Fokker D.I to D.V

Produced from mid-1916 to replace the Fokker E.III, the early D types were, on the whole, an undistinguished collection. Designed by Martin Kreutzer, the D.I to D.IV retained a similar basic fuselage to the E.III, allied to a new biplane wing cellule. Comparatively few in-line-engined D.Is and D.IVs were built; production of the rotary-engined D.II and D.III totalled two hundred and ninety-one.

The D.I, derived from the M.18Z prototype, was powered by a 120 h.p. Mercedes D.II and armed with a single forward-firing Spandau gun offset to port. The pilot's field of view was good, but the D.I, with its warp-controlled wings, was no match in manoeuvrability or climb for Allied Nieuports, and was quickly removed from the Western Front to Russia. At least one (04.41) was completed by M.A.G. in Austro-Hungary. The D.IV, with aileron control, was more manoeuvrable, but the additional output of its 160 h.p. Mercedes was offset to a great extent by the weight of a second gun and it offered little improvement over the D.I.

The rotary-engined models were rather better. The D.II, derived from the M.17Z, was probably built before the D.I, and also had warp-controlled wings and a single gun. Span was slightly shorter, but the fuselage was longer and fitted with a 100 h.p. Oberursel U.I in a 'horseshoe' cowling. No German squadrons were equipped fully with D.IIs, which were allocated in small batches to serve primarily as escorts. At least one D.II (04.51) was built in Austro-Hungary by M.A.G. To take the 160 h.p. U.III two-row rotary, the D.III had a strengthened airframe and the longer-span wings of the D.I, a deeper-chord cowling and modified undercarriage. It served briefly with a few Western Front *Jastas*, being flown by such pilots as Boelcke, von Richthofen and Udet. However, the U.III engine was an unreliable unit, and with the arrival of more effective fighters the D.III, in company with the other early Fokker D types, was withdrawn to training and miscellaneous duties. The D.III was also built by M.A.G. in Austro-Hungary. Some late-production German D.IIIs, including ten bought by the Dutch Army Air Service in 1917, were fitted with ailerons.

Before he was killed in a D.I in June 1916, Kreutzer developed a new prototype, the M.21, from the earlier M.17E. This was taken further by Platz to become the M.22, for which, in October 1916, came a production order as the D.V. This was a more shapely machine, with an entirely new wing cellule, a fully circular cowling for its 100 h.p. U.I engine and a hemispherical spinner. The D.V handled well, but its performance was inferior to the incoming Albatros fighters and it was transferred to a training role until the end of the war. A few D.Vs were used by the German Navy, possibly also for training.

49 Fokker D.VI

The little D.VI was not a fighter with any outstanding operational significance but it is of interest as a design link between the Dr.I triplane and the later D.VII. It had its origin in the V.9 prototype designed by Platz, which utilised a number of Dr.I components. The V.9 was developed into the V.13, two of which were completed late in 1917. Apart from simplified strutting, the most noticeable change was the more powerful engines, the V.13/1 having a 145 h.p. UR.III and the V.13/2 a 160 h.p. Sh.III. The fuselage and tail assembly were basically the same as those of the Dr.I, and the wings were a lower-aspect-ratio edition of those fitted to the Fokker D.VII. Despite the fairly wide gap between fuselage and upper wing the view from the cockpit was quite good.

Both V.13s took part in the Adlershof fighter trials in January/February 1918, and, despite the overall supremacy of the D.VII, a small order was also placed for the D.VI. Neither of the intended power plants was yet fully developed, and so production D.VIs were given 110 h.p. UR.IIs, which were a direct copy of the French Le Rhône. Between April and August 1918 forty-seven UR.II-powered D.VI were built, together with another dozen which had 200 h.p. Goe.IIIs. Only a few D.VIs saw service with front-line fighter units (including *Jasta* 84), and after the D.VII arrived in service the D.VI was transferred to training duties. The reason for this was certainly not due to any shortcomings in the D.VI which was a thoroughly manoeuvrable fighter and at low altitude was faster than the D.VII. The D.VI was armed with twin forward-firing Spandau guns mounted in front of the cockpit. Seven UR.II-powered

D.VIs which were supplied to Austro-Hungary in August 1918 may have been refitted with Schwarzlose guns after their arrival.

50   Hanriot HD.1

This attractive French single-seater, with its obvious Sopwith overtones, was a little unlucky in being overshadowed by its French contemporary, the Spad. The *Aviation Militaire* never used it operationally, and it was left to Belgian and Italian units to exploit its many qualities. René Hanriot, who had been a pioneer builder of fast, elegant and stable aeroplanes in France between 1910 and 1913, re-entered the aviation industry after the outbreak of war. He set up a new factory at Billancourt, where he was joined by Pierre Dupont; the first Hanriot-Dupont design, the HD.1, appeared in mid-1916. Bearing a close outward resemblance to the Sopwith Pup, the HD.1 was a very clean design with a minimum of external wires and cables and had the reliable 110 h.p. Le Rhône 9 J as its powerplant. France had already selected the heavier Spad VII to replace its Nieuport fighters, but great interest was shown in the HD.1 by the Italian Air Force, which was also seeking a Nieuport replacement. In general, Italian fighter pilots looked for manoeuvrability and good handling qualities first, stability and firepower second, and after testing the HD.1 extensively decided in late 1916 to adopt it as their new standard fighter. Work began in November at Nieuport-Macchi's Varese factory on an initial batch of a hundred HD.1s; after working up at training units the 76a *Squadriglia* became the first unit operational with HD.1s in August 1917. The HD.1 was armed with a single Vickers machine-gun on the port side of the upper decking. Italian pilots, however, found a central position more satisfactory, and this position was also adopted later by the Belgian *Aviation Militaire* on its HD.1s.

Total orders were placed for one thousand seven hundred HD.1s for the Italian Air Force, but rather less than half this number were finally delivered. Of the eight hundred and thirty-one accepted, some may have been French-built. Nevertheless, it remained the most widely used aircraft in Italian service for the rest of the war, and at its peak sixteen of Italy's eighteen fighter squadrons, including some based in Albania and Macedonia, were equipped with HD.1s. It remained in post-war service for several years, Nieuport-Macchi building a further seventy after the war; one *Stormo* still had HD.1s upon the formation of the *Regia Aeronautica* in 1923.

The other major service with HD.1s was the Belgian *Aviation Militaire*, which received one hundred and twenty-five French-built machines. The first order was placed in June 1917 and the first HD.1 was delivered on 22 August. Belgian pilots, like their Italian comrades, experimented with two-gun installations, but found the performance affected too much by the extra weight. A measure of the esteem in which the HD.1 was held is that

Belgium refused an offer of Sopwith Camels early in 1918 to replace its Hanriots, and the HD.1 continued with the Belgian Air Force until 1926.

The only HD.1s to see service with French forces were a few used as shipboard fighters by the *Aviation Maritime* in 1918. A twin-float version, the HD.2, appeared in 1918 and was built in small numbers. The HD.2 had a redesigned vertical tail, and some were fitted with twin Vickers guns. The U.S. Navy bought ten HD.2s late in 1918 for its coastal stations in France; these were later taken back to America and converted to landplanes. Sixteen HD.1s were sold to the Swiss *Fliegertruppe* in 1921.

51   Sopwith Pup

Developed by Herbert Smith from a personal aircraft flown by Harry Hawker in 1915, the Pup looked like a scaled-down offspring of the earlier $1\frac{1}{2}$-Strutter: hence its nickname, which persisted in spite of Admiralty orders to the contrary. The Pup was classically simple in appearance and construction, and had flying qualities which earned the descriptions 'perfect' and 'impeccable'. Its simplicity belied its ruggedness, and for 80 h.p. the Pup offered a remarkable performance and excellent manoeuvrability.

Although the bulk of later production was to R.F.C. orders, the Pup's origins and later associations lay mainly with the Royal Navy. The first of six prototypes was flown in February 1916, and the type underwent Admiralty service trials three months later. Initial orders were placed with Sopwith and Beardmore, and after the first few Beardmore machines the Le Rhône 9 C engine was standardised. R.N.A.S. Pups were referred to officially as Admiralty Type 9901 and were at first armed with one 0·303 in. Vickers gun mounted centrally in front of the pilot; these were synchronised with various gears throughout the Pup's service career. Eight Le Prieur rockets were an alternative armament, but were used comparatively little on Royal Navy Pups, although some were seen with rockets and a Vickers gun.

Deliveries commenced in autumn 1916, the first unit to receive Pups being No. 1 Wing R.N.A.S. Beardmore and Sopwith built one hundred and seventy Pups for the Navy, while Whitehead Aviation and the Standard Motor Co. completed a further one thousand six hundred and seventy for the R.F.C. Pups operated on the Western Front in late 1916/early 1917; in October 1916 the famous 'Naval 8' Squadron was formed to assist the R.F.C. Initially only one of No. 8's flights was equipped with Pups, but later all three flights (eighteen aircraft) had them. In the two final months of 1917 the Pups of No. 8 accounted for twenty enemy aircraft. From the beginning of 1918, although production had still not reached its peak, the Pup began to be withdrawn from front-line units; large numbers were transferred to raining establishments, where their qualities made them extremely popular.

Meanwhile, during 1917 the Pup had strengthened its association with the Fleet. Several were modified for shipboard anti-Zeppelin duties, with the Vickers gun replaced by a tripod-mounted Lewis n front of the cockpit, firing upward through a centre-section cut-out. Flight Commander F. J. Rutland did much experimental flying in the development of flotation bags for Naval Pups, and in pioneering take-offs from special platforms fitted to Naval cruisers. The first Pup to land on an aircraft carrier (H.M.S. *Furious*) performed this feat in the hands of Squadron Commander E. H. Dunning on 2 August 1917; this officer lost his life five days later while attempting his third landing-on. Much other valuable work was carried out at the Isle of Grain under the direction of Squadron Commander H. R. Busteed in connection with deck arrester equipment.

From July 1917 Pups also served with three R.F.C. and five R.N.A.S. Home Defence squadrons, many being fitted with 100 h.p. Gnome Monosoupape engines and a few with 80 h.p. Gnomes. However, they had neither the range nor the altitude to deal satisfactorily with the attacking German bombers. Altogether, Pups were carried by five aircraft carriers and seven Royal Navy cruisers during 1914–18. A development of the Pup with folding, unstaggered wings and a slightly longer fuselage was evolved

by Beardmore as the W.B.III: thirteen of these were built as S.B.3F (Folding undercarriage) and eighty-seven as S.B.3D (Dropping – i.e. jettisonable – undercarriage), but in general they were less popular and their handling qualities inferior to the standard Pup.

After the war the Pup disappeared quickly from the British scene. Only eight found their way to the civil register, all of which had disappeared by 1924. Eleven were supplied to the Royal Australian Air Force in 1919, and small numbers also went to the United States, Greece, the Netherlands and Russia.

52 Airco D.H.5

The least successful de Havilland design of 1914–18, the D.H.5 was operational for only eight months. It was an attempt to combine the excellent all-round view of the D.H.2 with the higher performance of a tractor biplane layout. This was accomplished by giving the wings a backward stagger so as to seat the pilot ahead of the upper wing. The prototype (A5172), completed late in 1916, was powered by a 110 h.p. Le Rhône engine. It underwent official trials in December, being sent to France later that month for service trials with a forward-firing Vickers gun. By this time the vertical tail had been modified to a contour similar to that of the D.H.4.

Production aircraft differed in having an octagonal-section rear fuselage instead of a slab-sided one. The machine-gun fitted to the prototype had been installed to elevate to approximately 60 degrees, but production D.H.5s had a fixed forward-firing 0·303 in. Vickers with Constantinesco interrupter gear. The Aircraft Manufacturing Co. built one hundred and ninety-nine D.H.5s in addition to the prototype; a further two hundred were ordered from the Darracq Motor Engineering Co., one hundred from March, Jones & Cribb, and fifty from the British Caudron Co. First deliveries were made to Nos. 24 and 32 Squadrons in May 1917, where they replaced the D.H.2; in July No. 41 Squadron replaced its F.E.8s with D.H.5s; and in the autumn two new squadrons – Nos. 64 and 68 (Australian No. 2) – were formed with D.H.5s.

There was much prejudice against the D.H.5 when it reached France. Crews were suspicious of its unconventional appearance, and convinced that it was dangerous to fly. These fears were largely unfounded, but the D.H.5's mediocre performance at heights above 10,000 ft. (3,048 m.) prevented it from becoming a very effective fighter. On the other hand, its sturdy construction and good low-level performance made it a useful ground-attack aircraft, for which purpose it could carry four 25 lb. Cooper bombs under the fuselage. It was used thus at the Battle of Cambrai in autumn 1917, though by this time its withdrawal had begun in favour of the S.E.5a. By January 1918 all D.H.5s had been withdrawn to Schools of Aerial Fighting and the Advanced Air Firing School in the United Kingdom. Here, too, the D.H.5

suffered several landing and other accidents and became as unpopular as it had been in France, and by 31 October 1918 no D.H.5s remained on R.A.F. charge.

Experimental variants included at least two aircraft with Clerget and Gnome Monosoupape engines; another was delivered to the Royal Aircraft Factory; and one (A9186) was, like the prototype, fitted with an upward-angled Vickers gun, and may have been intended as an anti-Zeppelin fighter.

53   Vickers F.B.19

The Aviation Department of Vickers Ltd. was noted chiefly during 1914-18 for its series of 'gunbus' pusher biplanes, but in August 1915 it brought out a prototype single-seat tractor biplane scout known as the E.S.1. Powered by a 100 h.p. Gnome Monosoupape engine, the E.S.1 reached 114 m.p.h. at 5,000 ft. (183 km/hr. at 1,524 m.), and was followed in September by the E.S.2 which had a 110 h.p. Le Rhône. Neither of these entered production, and a year elapsed before, in August 1916, the F.B.19 appeared. This bore a close resemblance to the E.S.1 and E.S.2, although its Monosoupape was less carefully cowled and the wingtips were slightly raked. A single 0·303 in. synchronised Vickers machine-gun was mounted in front of the cockpit, slightly offset to port. A drawback to the 1915 scouts had been the poor view from the cockpit, due to the unstaggered wings, and some attempt to improve this was made by incorporating a large rectangular cut-out in the middle of the F.B.19's top wing.

In November 1916 the first production F.B.19s appeared, having 110 h.p. Le Rhônes in shallower cowlings and a small headrest behind the cockpit. The first few were designated F.B.19 Mk.I, but these seem to have been replaced almost immediately by the Mk.II, in which the wings were given a marked forward stagger to improve both the pilot's view and the aerodynamic qualities. The Vickers gun in the Mk.II was recessed in a trough about half-way down the port side of the fuselage and, with Challenger synchronising gear, fired through a small hole in the engine cowling to the left of the propeller shaft.

Sixty-five F.B.19s were built by Vickers' Weybridge factory. Thirty-six were issued to the R.F.C., the first six being sent to France before the end of 1916 for operational assessment. A few were delivered to Russia at about this time, but the F.B.19 was not accepted for service on the Western Front. Five were allocated to Nos. 14 and 111 Squadrons in Palestine in June 1917, and seven others to 17 and 47 Squadrons in Macedonia, but their combat career appears to have been uneventful. Of the remainder, six went to Home Defence squadrons and twelve to training units in the United Kingdom during the second half of 1917. It is unlikely that many survived the war; one was registered to Vickers as G-EAAU in May 1919, but the registration was cancelled two months later, suggesting that this aircraft was never civilianised.

54 Thomas-Morse S-4

The Thomas-Morse Aircraft Corporation was formed in January 1917 by the English-born Thomas brothers with backing from the Morse Chain Co. Its chief designer, B. D. Thomas (no relation), had previously played a large part in designing the Curtiss 'Jenny'. Early in 1917 he designed a single-seat trainer, the S-4, which flew for the first time in June. This was accepted by the U.S. Army as the S-4B, subject to various changes including a 2 ft. 9 in. (0·94 m.) shorter fuselage and smaller control surfaces.

In October 1917 the Signal Corps ordered a hundred S-4Bs for advanced flying training. Apart from a tail-heavy tendency the S-4B's flying qualities were generally good, but trouble was experienced with oil leakages and other shortcomings of the 100 h.p. Gnome Monosoupape engine, and when four hundred improved S-4Cs were ordered in January 1918 it was decided to use the more reliable 80 h.p. Le Rhône 9 C, although the first fifty S-4Cs were completed with Monosoupapes. Other changes included less wing stagger and smaller control areas. Provision existed for a 0·30 in. Marlin machine-gun in front of the cockpit on the starboard side; alternatively, a camera gun could be fitted. In August and October 1918 further orders for one hundred and fifty and five hundred S-4Cs were placed, but after the Armistice the latter contract was cancelled and only ninety-seven of the August order were completed. The S-4's tail heaviness was never eradicated entirely, but its general flying qualities were much better than those of the more widespread 'Jenny', and it was extremely manoeuvrable. The S-4 was employed solely in the United States, mostly by the Signal Corps, but the U.S. Navy received ten ex-Army S-4Bs and S-4Cs, and six twin-float S-5s which were otherwise similar to the S-4B. Final wartime variant, and the last single-seat 'Tommy', was the S-4E of 1918. This had shorter-span, tapered wings and a faster speed, but remained a prototype.

Many war-surplus S-4s appeared on the civil market after the Armistice, enjoying a new career as private-owner and racing aircraft for several years. Many were re-engined with 110 h.p. Le Rhônes or 90 h.p. Curtiss OX-5s, and several others were assembled from wartime spares. The S-4 enjoyed considerable use by Hollywood in films such as *Hell's Angels*, in which it often represented wartime British, French or German fighters. Post-war variants included the S-6, S-7 and S-9 (there is no record of an S-8). The S-6 and S-7 appeared in January 1919, the former having two seats in tandem and the latter two side-by-side seats. The S-9 was a tandem 2-seater with a 200 h.p. Wright J-3 radial engine.

55   Standard E-1

The aircraft built by the Standard Aircraft Corporation during the latter part of the 1914–18 war were certainly an assorted collection, for they ranged in size from single-engined D.H.4s to giant Caproni and Handley Page bombers. The company also built substantial numbers of the SJ-1, a 2-seat trainer of its own design bearing a close resemblance to the Curtiss 'Jenny'. Its first fighter venture was the E-1, designed in 1917. This was a neat little rotary-engined machine with lines reminiscent of some of the later Sopwith products. Two prototypes were delivered in January 1918, each powered by an 80 h.p. Le Rhône 9 C engine and having a blunt, rounded spinner over the propeller hub. A single 0·30 in. Marlin machine-gun was offset to port in front of the cockpit, with provision for a camera gun in the corresponding position to starboard.

An initial sixty Le Rhône-powered E-1s were built in 1918 as 'M-Defense' fighters: delivery of these began in November, followed by a further seventy-five E-1s with similar powerplants. They were preceded from August 1918 by thirty-three E-1s having redesigned vertical tail surfaces and 100 h.p. Gnome 9 B engines; but even with the higher-rated engines the E-1 was under-powered and too slow for fighting, and the type was employed instead as an advanced trainer, of which four hundred and sixty were ordered. Standard produced a project study later in 1918 for a new fighter with a 300 h.p. engine, but this was abandoned after the war ended. Three E-1s were converted in post-war years by Sperry to radio-controlled flying bombs known as MATs (Messenger Aerial Torpedoes).

Although it never achieved the same eminence, the Siemens-Schuckert fighter was, in terms of power, manoeuvrability and rate of climb, the nearest parallel to the Sopwith Camel produced by the German aviation industry during 1914–18. In 1917 another member of the great Siemens combine, the Siemens-Halske engine works, produced a new rotary engine, the 11-cylinder Sh.III, which offered 160 h.p. Under the direction of Dipl. Ing. Harald Wolff three prototype machines, designated D.II, D.IIa and D.IIb, were built around this powerplant and began flight tests in June 1917. The D.II was not outstandingly fast, but it had an excellent climb. Three more development aircraft were ordered, a short-span and a long-span D.IIc and a standard-span D.IIe. These, completed in October, were later redesignated D.III. Twenty D.IIIs were ordered in December 1917, with smaller, 4-blade propellers and shorter undercarriage legs. Delivery began in January 1918; in February thirty more D.IIIs were ordered, and by the end of May delivery to front-line *Jastas*, notably Nos. 12 and 15, was almost complete. The fully cowled Sh.III had a tendency to overheat, and in the early summer the D.IIIs were returned to the factory for minor airframe alterations and installation of 200 h.p. Sh.IIIa engines. They were returned to service from July onward, having the lower part of the cowling cut away to

facilitate cooling. By this time their primary value was as home defence fighters, in which role they were highly successful. Eighty D.IIIs were built altogether, serving with *Jastas* 2, 12, 13, 15, 19, 26, 27 and 36, with five home defence units and one or two training establishments.

Meanwhile the long-span D.IIc had been further refined, and with narrower-chord wings became the forerunner of the D.IV. The D.IV was faster in level flight and even better in a climb than the D.III, and was ordered in March 1918. It became operational in the following August. An eventual two hundred and eighty D.IVs were ordered, but only one hundred and twenty-three were completed. About half of these had reached front-line units (including *Jastas* 11, 14 and 22) by the Armistice. The D.IV was rather tricky to land, but in all other respects was an admirable aeroplane. It had a very short take-off, and at heights above 4,000 m. (13,123 ft.) was faster and more manoeuvrable than the Fokker D.VIII. Its outstanding feature was its phenomenal rate of climb – it could reach 6,000 m. (19,685 ft.) in less than $14\frac{1}{2}$ minutes. As late as October 1918 it was officially described as 'superior by far to all single-seaters in use at the Front today'.

Production of the D.IV did not finally end until summer 1919. In 1918 a 2-bay derivative, the D.V, participated in the Adlershof trials in May/June, but was not built in quantity.

57 Sopwith Camel

The Camel, evolved by Herbert Smith to succeed the Pup and triplane, had none of the docile handling qualities of its predecessors, and had to be mastered before it could be flown successfully. That it was flown successfully is demonstrated by the fact that Camels were credited with destroying more enemy aircraft than any other Allied type. Aided by the torque from its heavy rotary engine, the Camel could out-turn any German fighter, except possibly the Fokker Dr.I. Like the Pup, its name was originally an unofficial one, derived from the humped appearance created by the fairing over the breeches of its twin Vickers guns.

The prototype appeared in December 1916, powered by a 110 h.p. Clerget 9 Z. A further small batch was completed, including two for the Admiralty and one with a 130 h.p. Clerget. Production Camels were based on the latter aircraft, at first having either Clerget 9 Bs or 150 h.p. Bentley B.R.1s; deliveries began in May 1917. The first unit to receive Camels was No. 4 Squadron R.N.A.S., with whom they became operational in July. Concurrent R.F.C. orders specified either the Clerget 9 B, B.R.1 or 110 h.p. Le Rhône 9 J engine. Camels were fitted with twin Vickers guns in front of the cockpit; synchronising gear varied according to the engine fitted. Clerget Camels were on the whole faster, though they had a less efficient synchronising gear; the Le Rhône Camels, with the better Constantinesco gear, had a

faster climb. By July 1917 first R.F.C. deliveries had been made to No. 70 Squadron, and by the end of the year one thousand three hundred and twenty-five Camels (of three thousand four hundred and fifty then on order) had been delivered. They were used widely for ground attack during the Battles of Ypres and Cambrai, with four 20 lb. Cooper bombs under the fuselage. Heavy losses among ground-attack Camels led to the appearance of the armour-plated TF.1 (Trench Fighter No. 1); this did not enter production, but it yielded much valuable information towards the later TF.2 Salamander. A few Camels, presumably for training, had 100 h.p. Monosoupape engines. One hundred and forty-three Clerget-powered Camels were purchased in June 1918 by the United States. These were later re-engined – to their detriment – with 150 h.p. Monosoupapes, and issued to four A.E.F. squadrons. From August 1917 the Le Rhône Camel was employed for Home Defence duties, with twin Lewis guns on a Foster mounting over the centre-section and the cockpit resited aft of the trailing edge.

All Camels so far discussed were F.1 landplane fighters, but a shipboard version, the 2F.1, underwent official trials in March 1917. Although visually similar, it differed in construction from the F.1, having a 1 ft. 1 in. (0·33 m.) shorter span and the starboard Vickers deleted in favour of an upward-angled Lewis firing through a small centre-section cut-out. One hundred and eighty-nine 2F.1 Camels were built, but they did not become operational until spring 1918. Powerplants remained the Clerget 9 B or the B.R.1, and some 2F.1s acted as dive-bombers with two 50 lb. bombs under the fuselage. By the end of the war 2F.1 Camels had served aboard five aircraft carriers, two battleships and twenty-six cruisers of the Royal Navy.

Discounting prototypes and cancelled contracts, five thousand four hundred and ninety Camels were ordered, though delivery of all of these has not been established; neither is it certain whether this figure includes the 2F.1 total. On 31 October 1918 the R.A.F. had two thousand five hundred and forty-eight F.1s on charge, over half of them with Clerget engines, and one hundred and twenty-nine 2F.1s. The Camel did not remain long in post-war R.A.F. service, being replaced by the Snipe, but it continued to serve for some years with the Belgian *Aviation Militaire*, the Canadian Air Force, the Royal Hellenic Naval Air Service, the Polish Air Force and the U.S. Navy; and two came on to the British civil register. Camel variants which appeared during the war included the Sopwith Scooter (June 1918) and Swallow (October 1918). These were parasol monoplanes, the Scooter being a personal aircraft developed for Harry Hawker and the Swallow a fighter project.

58 Sopwith Salamander

Mention has already been made in the description of the Sopwith Camel of the experimental TF.1 (Trench Fighter): no production of this was undertaken, but it provided valuable knowledge for the evolution of the Sopwith TF.2 Salamander, which flew on 27 April 1918. This was the first of three prototypes, and was sent to France the following month for service evaluation. The design of the Salamander was generally the same as that of the 7F.1 Snipe, retaining the same big two-row rotary in a cowling cut away underneath to improve cooling. Two 0·303 in. Vickers machine-guns, each with 1,000 rounds of ammunition, were synchronised with Constantinesco gear to fire between the propeller blades, and the pilot's position and fuel tanks were encased in armour plating which contributed 650 lb. (295 kg.) towards the aircraft's gross weight. Four 25 lb. Cooper bombs could be carried beneath the fuselage.

The evolution of aircraft for specialised ground-attack duties had assumed an important role during the final year of the war, and plans were made for large-scale production of the Salamander. Five hundred were ordered from Sopwith and six hundred more from five other manufacturers. However, when all outstanding contracts were cancelled after the Armistice only one hundred and two Sopwith-built machines had been completed; only thirty-seven of these were on R.A.F. charge on 31 October 1918, and only two had arrived in France. Sopwith production continued, however, well into 1919, the eventual total built being one hundred and sixty or more. One Salamander was taken to the United States for further study. As described in Appendix 1, the third prototype was one of four types of aircraft to carry out flight trials painted in camouflage schemes drawn up for observation aircraft by the Ministry of Munitions.

59 Sopwith Snipe

The Snipe came into being to replace the Camel, with improved performance and outlook from the cockpit. Six prototypes were ordered in the late summer of 1917: the first was completed with a 150 h.p. Bentley B.R.1 engine and Camel-type tail. Several modifications were made after installing the more powerful B.R.2, but the Snipe at last went into production in spring 1918. Standard armament was two synchronised Vickers guns mounted in front of the cockpit. Experiments were conducted with a third gun, a Lewis, mounted above the top wing, but this proved difficult to operate, and its weight had an adverse effect on the Snipe's performance.

Initial contracts in March 1918 called for one thousand seven hundred Snipes from Sopwith and six other manufacturers. Deliveries started in mid-1918, and by 30 September one hundred and sixty-one Snipe Mk.Is had been delivered. The Snipe became operational in September with No. 43 Squadron R.A.F., and in October with No. 208 Squadron and No. 4 Squadron Australian Flying Corps. Two long range Mk.Ias were

allocated to No. 45 Squadron to serve with the Independent Force. Snipes were generally used for escort work, but could carry four 20 lb. Cooper bombs beneath the fuselage. On 31 October 1918 two were on Royal Navy charge and a further ninety-seven on R.A.F. charge; one of the latter, serving with a Home Defence unit, presaged the selection of the Snipe as a standard night fighter in 1919.

Additional contracts brought total Snipe orders to four thousand five hundred and fifteen, but there were heavy cancellations after the Armistice and little more than one-third of these were actually completed before production ceased in March 1919. Snipes served with many peacetime R.A.F. squadrons at home and overseas, and with Nos. 37, 78, 112 and 143 Squadrons in the night-fighter role. Several were stationed in Germany after the Armistice as part of the occupation force. Some were converted to 2-seat unarmed trainers. In 1924 the Snipe was replaced by the Gloster Grebe. A few civil Snipes were flown in Britain, Canada and the United States. A variant intended for large-scale production was the Dragon, with a 320 h.p. A.B.C. Dragonfly radial engine, but this unit proved unsatisfactory and the Dragon did not go into service with the R.A.F.

60 Sopwith triplane

The delightful little triplane, evolved by Herbert Smith to wring even more manoeuvrability from the basic design which had yielded the Pup, appeared in unarmed prototype form late in May 1916 and was test-flown by Harry Hawker. Power-plant was a 110 h.p. Clerget 9 Z. With a centrally mounted Vickers gun, and bearing the serial number N500, the prototype was tested in France by the R.N.A.S. in June 1916, where its outstanding performance resulted in immediate orders from both the Admiralty and the War Office. The combined orders originally totalled just over four hundred: in October the Navy traded its available Spad VIIs to meet an urgent R.F.C. requirement in return for a promise of all triplanes on order for the R.F.C. but only ninety-five were completed by Sopwith, plus forty-six by Clayton & Shuttleworth and three by Oakley Ltd.

Meanwhile, a second prototype (N504) had been flown with a 130 h.p. Clerget 9 B, and this became the standard installation. The single Vickers was retained, with a Scarff–Dibovski synchronising gear, though a few aircraft are known to have been fitted with twin Vickers guns. Triplane deliveries started around November 1916, ultimately going to Nos. 1, 8, 9, 10, 11 and 12 Squadrons R.N.A.S. on the Western Front; Nos. 1, 8 and 10 were attached to the R.F.C. during most of 1917. The triplane's successes, due largely to its outstanding agility and climb, created such an impact in enemy circles that fourteen German and Austrian manufacturers built triplane 'answers' to the Sopwith fighter. Introduced at a time when the Albatros D.I/D.II fighters were coming into service, the Sopwith triplane retained its superiority even over the later D.III and D.V, and had still not been outclassed when it began to be replaced by the Camel in summer 1917. By the end of the year most triplanes had been withdrawn to training or experimental duties. From February 1917, modifications to aircraft in production and service reduced the size of the horizontal tail to enhance the aircraft's diving ability.

The triplane served almost exclusively on the Western Front, but during 1917, in addition to six aircraft delivered to the French government, another was flown with the Imperial Russian Air Service (on a ski landing gear) and one was sent to the United States. One served with No. 2 Wing R.N.A.S. in the Aegean, and here also Flt. Lt. J. W. Alcock (the transatlantic Vimy pilot of 1919) built his own 'one-off' Alcock A.1 scout from triplane components. Two other single-seat triplane fighters were built by Sopwith: these were apparently based on the 1½-Strutter and powered respectively by 150 and 200 h.p. Hispano-Suiza Vee-type engines. Neither was developed beyond the prototype stage.

61 Fokker Dr.I

Such was the impact created in German military circles by the Sopwith triplane that, apparently believing that the triple-wing arrangement was a magic formula for success, no fewer than fourteen German and Austrian manufacturers produced triplane designs of their own. Most of them did so after inspecting a captured British machine in July 1917, but they were well behind Anthony Fokker, who had seen the Sopwith in action at the Front in April. It has often been implied that the Fokker Dr.I was a copy of the Sopwith triplane, but Reinhold Platz, who designed the Fokker machine at his employer's request, had never seen the British aeroplane, and indeed was quite unconvinced of the merits of a triplane layout.

Nevertheless, he produced a prototype known as the V.3 with three sets of cantilever wings, the only struts being those on which the top plane was mounted. Single, thin interplane struts and balanced ailerons, together with two 7·92 mm. Spandaus, were added after the V.3 had been test-flown by Fokker, and in this form it became the V.4. In virtually unchanged form two further prototypes and three hundred and eighteen Dr.Is were ordered in summer 1917. Following acceptance trials in August, the second and third prototypes became operational with von Richthofen's *Jagdgeschwader I*. The third machine was flown almost exclusively by Leutnant Werner Voss, who scored his first victory with it on 30 August. In the next twenty-four days Voss scored a further twenty victories before being shot down and killed on 23 September by an S.E.5a of No. 56 Squadron. From mid-October, deliveries of production Dr.Is began to JG.I, but by early November a series of fatal crashes caused them to be grounded. The trouble

was faulty workmanship in the wing construction, and for most of the remainder of November the Fokker factory was occupied in repairing or replacing the defective wings. The Dr.I thus did not become fully operational until late November, and its subsequent career at the Front was brief. Nevertheless, it achieved considerable success, due mainly to its excellent manoeuvrability. It was in a Fokker Dr.I that, on 21 April 1918, the legendary Manfred von Richthofen was finally shot down and killed. The Dr. I reached its peak of service early in May 1918, when one hundred and seventy-one were in front-line service. Later that month production ceased, and thereafter the Dr.I was transferred to home defence until the Armistice, at which time sixty-nine were in service.

The standard powerplant of the Dr.I was the 110 h.p. Oberursel UR.II or Goebel Goe.II rotary. Some aircraft had the 200 h.p. Goe. III or IIIa engine or the 110 h.p. French-built (captured) or copied Le Rhône; experimental installations included the Sh.III and captured 130 h.p. Clergets. In 1917 Platz produced an alternative triplane prototype, the V.6, which had a 120 h.p. Mercedes D.II stationary engine, but the V.6 proved more clumsy than the rotary-engined Dr.I, and no further examples were built.

62 Morane-Saulnier AI

Two similar single-seat Morane-Saulnier designs appeared during the first half of 1917; the AF, a biplane, did not achieve production or service status, but the monoplane AI, although it did not enjoy a particularly successful wartime career, was produced in substantial numbers and set a pattern that was followed by subsequent Morane-Saulnier fighters until the early 1930s. It was produced in three versions for the French *Aviation Militaire*, all having sweptback parasol wings with a large 'V' cut-out in the trailing edge. For the fighter role the AI could be fitted with one or two 0·303 in. Vickers machine-guns on top of the engine cowling; military designations were MoS.27C.1 for the single-gun version and MoS.29C.1 for the two-gun version. Both were powered by the 150 h.p. Gnome Monosoupape. A third model, the MoS.30E.1, was produced for advanced training, usually with a 120 or 135 h.p. Le Rhône engine.

First deliveries of the AI were made towards the end of 1917, and in January 1918 it became operational with *Escadrille* 156. Four months later the type had been withdrawn from combat duty and transferred entirely to the training role. Among the reasons advanced for this were faults with the Monosoupape engine and allegations that the aeroplane was suspect structurally. The latter claim seems unlikely, and it may simply have been the superiority of the Spad fighters which brought the AI's operational life to an early close. Of the one thousand two hundred and ten aircraft built, three MoS.30s were supplied in 1918 to the Belgian *Aviation Militaire*, and

fifty-one MoS.30s to the American Expeditionary Force.

The AI remained in service as an aerobatic trainer for some time after the end of the war, some MoS.30s being re-engined with the 130 h.p. Clerget 9 Ba rotary. Some AIs found their way to Japan, Russia and Spain, and several came on to the French civil register, one of the most notable being F-NUNG, a Clerget-engined MoS.30 in which Charles Nungesser took part in many postwar air displays until the mid-1920s. This aircraft was decorated with the familiar 'death's head' emblem carried by Nungesser on his wartime Nieuport 17. Allegations of structural weakness in the basic design were answered convincingly by the performance of MM. Fronval and Joyce, of whom the former in 1922 put an aeroplane of this type through no fewer than 1,111 consecutive loops.

63 Morane-Saulnier L, LA and P

Over a period of two decades Morane-Saulnier produced a string of parasol monoplane fighters. The first of them all, which appeared in 1913, was the Type L (military designation MoS.3). This was a simple and rather frail-looking aeroplane with a box-like fuselage and an 80 h.p. Gnome or Le Rhône 9 C rotary engine in a 'horseshoe' cowling. Lateral control was by wing-warping.

Upon the outbreak of war the Type L was ordered in large numbers, the intention being to use it for reconnaissance; but it was appreciably faster than German 2-seaters then in service, and crews were encouraged to take small-arms with them in the cockpit. The most common weapon was the cavalry carbine, with which considerable success was achieved. France's Georges Guynemer scored his first aerial victory in an MoS.3 in July 1915.

It was a Morane Type L (and not a Type N, as was believed for many years) which unwittingly brought about the so-called Fokker 'scourge' of 1915–16. Some two months before the war Raymond Saulnier had experimented with an interrupter mechanism to enable a machine-gun mounted in front of the pilot to fire between the blades of a propeller without hitting them. He achieved a limited success with some static tests, but at the end of the year was joined by the French pilot Roland Garros, who instead fitted steel deflector plates to turn aside any stray bullets that struck the propeller blades. In March 1915 Garros returned to his unit (MS.26) with a Morane L fitted with a forward-firing 8 mm. Hotchkiss machine-gun and deflector plates on both propeller blades. Garros quickly made use of the surprise value of his unique weapon, and in the first three weeks of April scored three victories; but on 18 April he had to force-land behind enemy lines and was unable to destroy his aircraft completely before it was captured. This incident provided the spur which resulted in the successful interrupter gear developed by Fokker's engineers and

introduced on the E type monoplanes later that year.

The Type L gave excellent service in its intended reconnaissance role, and was also used for light bombing and agent-dropping. Nearly six hundred were built, serving widely with the French *Aviation Militaire*, No. 3 Squadron R.F.C. and No. 1 Wing R.N.A.S. in France, with No. 2 Wing R.N.A.S. in the Aegean, and with the Imperial Russian Air Service. It was in a Morane Type L that Flt. Sub-Lt. R. A. J. Warneford of the R.N.A.S. won the V.C. for the first destruction of a Zeppelin (LZ. 37) by an aircraft in the air. The six 25 lb. bombs carried by Warneford's aircraft on this occasion were typical of the load of the Morane L when used for light bombing.

A developed version, the LA, appeared in 1914. This had a rounded fuselage, aileron control, small fins above and below the rear fuselage and an airscrew spinner; it had the military designation MoS.4. Comparatively little use seems to have been made of the LA by the French, though it served in small numbers until the arrival of the Nieuport 11. Twenty-four LAs were supplied to the R.F.C., serving with Nos. 1 and 3 Squadrons in 1916–17. A more widespread version was the Type P, basically an enlarged LA with more power, a Lewis gun in the rear cockpit and, on later aircraft, a synchronised forward-firing Vickers gun. This appeared in two forms: the MoS.21, with a Le Rhône 9 J, and the MoS.26, with a Le Rhône 9 Jb. Like the L and LA, it was a

2-seater, and served with both the *Aviation Militaire* and the R.F.C. in 1916–17; five hundred and sixty-five Type Ps were built.

64 Fokker E.V/D.VIII

Reinhold Platz designed and built several shoulder-wing monoplanes from late 1917. His first parasol monoplanes were the rotary-engined V.26 and V.28 and the stationary-engined V.27, which took part in the second fighter competition at Adlershof in May/June 1918.

A refreshingly simple design, it had a one-piece cantilever wing and twin Spandau guns mounted immediately in front of the cockpit. Following their performance at Adlershof, the V.26/28 design was accepted for production and an initial four hundred were ordered with the *Eindecker* designation E.V. It was proposed to use either the 145 h.p. UR.III or the 200 h.p. Goe.III, but since these were not yet available in quantity, the early E.Vs had either Thulin-built Le Rhônes or Oberursel UR.IIs of 110 h.p. Differing only in rounder wingtips, which slightly increased the span, production E.Vs began to be delivered from July 1918. In August *Jasta* 6, one of the first units to receive E.Vs, experienced three serious crashes due to wing failure, and it looked as if the defects of the Fokker Dr.I were appearing in the E.V. Sixty or so aircraft were withheld pending investigations that ultimately vindicated Platz's design by revealing that the failures were due to poor workmanship and the use of imperfect timber by the contractor who had built the wing units. With the resumption of production in September 1918 the type was redesignated D.VIII and began to reach the Front towards the end of October. It thus had little chance to prove its worth, but reports indicate that it flew well, was more manoeuvrable than the D.VII and might well have replaced it. Although only eighty-five E.V/D.VIIIs were in service with front-line *Jastas* on 1 November 1918 (plus some with Naval fighter units), it seems that the full four hundred were probably built. Twenty formed part of Anthony Fokker's famous 'salvage act' of aircraft and engines smuggled into Holland, where some later served with the Dutch Army Air Service for several years, eventually with 145 h.p. UR.III engines. Small numbers of D.VIIIs went as spoils of war to Britain, France, Italy and the United States; others went to the Polish Air Force, where they were again used in combat early in 1919 against the Ukrainian forces, and to Japan. At the final Adlershof competition in October 1918 the joint winner was another parasol prototype, the V.29. This was based on the D.VII airframe and powered by a 185 h.p. B.M.W. IIIa.

65 Etrich Taube (Dove)

The Austrian engineer Igo Etrich designed and flew his first tractor monoplane on 20 July 1909, and the first *Taube* prototype in July 1910. In late 1910 Etrich negotiated a manufacturing licence with Lohner in Austria and Rumpler in Germany, and the latter company produced most of the *Tauben* built from then until the outbreak of World War I. Those built from 1911 onward reflected a host of dimensional and other variations, but the 2-seat military version produced by Rumpler in 1912 was the most widespread and may be taken as typical.

At the outbreak of war in Europe on 4 August 1914 *Tauben* were already in service with the air forces of Italy, Germany and Austria-Hungary as observation and training aircraft, and many later-famous German pilots learned to fly on aircraft of this type. Privately owned *Tauben* were impressed for military service, and a large-scale production programme was put in hand. By this time Dr. Etrich had relinquished his copyright in the design, following a dispute with Rumpler, and this left the way clear for *Tauben* for various types to be built in Germany by the Albatros, D.F.W., Gotha, Halberstadt, Jeannin, Kondor, Krieger, L.V.G., Lübeck-Travemünde and Rumpler factories. Etrich, meanwhile, joined forces with industrialist Gottfried Krüger in early 1914 to form the Brandenburgische (later Hansa-und-Brandenburgische) Flugzeugwerke G.m.b.H. About five hundred *Tauben* were built in Germany, those by D.F.W. and Jeannin being known as *Stahltauben* because of their steel-framed fuselages. A wide variety of engines, with output ranging from 70 to 120 h.p., were fitted to German-built machines, the most popular units being the Mercedes or Argus in-lines of 100 or 120 h.p. The two ver-sions in Austro-Hungarian service were the Lohner-built A.I (with 85 h.p. Austro-Daimler and overhead radiators) and the A.II (120 h.p. Austro-Daimler with frontal radiator), built by Lohner and (as the Series 71 and 72) by the K.u.K. Flieger Arsenal at Fischamend.

In August 1914 the *Taube* quickly proved its worth as a reconnaissance aircraft when it gave the Germans warning of a Russian advance during the Battle of Tannenburg. Later that month it was used for bombing when Lt. von Hiddesen dropped a small load of tiny bombs on Paris. The *Taube* was a stable aircraft with pleasant flying characteristics, and considering that it was already four years old when war broke out, its performance for 1914–15 was not at all bad. However, it was not highly manoeuvrable, and since it carried no armament (other than crew members' revolvers or rifles), it was of little front-line value by the spring of 1915. It remained in use for a year or more thereafter as a very useful training type.

66 Morane-Saulnier N

Sometimes referred to, incorrectly, as the 'Monocoque Morane', the Type N monoplane was one of the best wartime products of Robert and Léon Morane and Raymond Saulnier. When it appeared in June 1914 it was an extremely advanced design for its time. Its circular-section fuselage, combined with its huge domed spinner, gave it a highly streamlined appearance, and it was extremely manoeuvrable. It was very sensitive on the controls, and with its rather high landing speed was not an aeroplane to be flown by a novice.

Only forty-nine Type Ns are thought to have been built: they received the official designation MoS.6C.1 in French service, where they were used by *escadrilles* MS. 12, 23, 38 and 49. Twenty-four were ordered by the R.F.C., with whose Nos. 1, 3, 24 and 60 Squadrons the Type N also served; these were known familiarly as 'Bullets'. Standard powerplant was the 80 h.p. Le Rhône 9 C rotary engine. Modifications introduced on some later aircraft included a strengthened undercarriage, revised engine cowling and smaller spinner. The original large spinners of the Morane N were apparently a source of trouble, for while they improved the aerodynamics of the fighter they also hampered the engine cooling system and were often left off operational aircraft. Most of the examples in French service were armed with a single 0·303 in. Vickers machine-gun fitted with an interrupter gear, while those of the R.F.C. were fitted with a 0·303 in. Lewis. No. 60 Squadron also operated four examples of the Type I and eight of the Type V, both developed versions of the Type N. A few Type Ns were supplied to the 19th Squadron of the Imperial Russian Air Service.

As well as possessing an effective armament, the Type N showed a good turn of speed and could climb to 3,000 m. (9,843 ft.) in 12 minutes. In 1916 a developed version appeared, known as the Type AC

(military designation MoS.23C.1). This was a slightly larger aircraft than the Type N and differed principally in having rigid underwing bracing and a 120 h.p. Le Rhône engine. Armament consisted of one synchronised Vickers machine-gun. Thirty-one Type ACs were built, one of them being used for an experimental installation of twin synchronised Vickers guns; it is doubtful if the AC saw much, if any, operational service.

67 Bristol M.1C

One of the most unlucky aeroplanes of 1914–18, the Bristol M.1C was condemned to virtual obscurity when there was a crying need on the Western Front for a fighter of its calibre. In October 1912 a committee was set up to investigate crashes by R.F.C. monoplanes; and although this body did not officially condemn monoplanes as such, a prejudice against them persisted throughout the war. F. S. Barnwell of the British and Colonial Aeroplane Co. still believed that a monoplane would achieve a higher performance than a biplane, and this was convincingly proved by his M.1A prototype (A5138), which reached 132 m.p.h. (212 km/hr.) during trials, powered by a 110 h.p. Clerget 9 Z rotary engine. Four M.1Bs differed from the M.1A in having a pyramid cabane instead of two half-hoops, a single Vickers gun offset to port and a cut-out in the starboard wing root to improve the view downward. Two were powered by 110 h.p. Clergets, the third M.1B having a 130 h.p. Clerget 9 B and the fourth a 150 h.p. A.R.1. The M.1Bs were used for service trials, the third and fourth aircraft going to the Middle East in June 1917, where they were used on operations. One of the others may have been used in France.

At this point the anti-monoplane faction exercised its influence. Hard-pressed fighter squadrons, eagerly awaiting delivery of the 'Bristol Bullets', heard that the War Office had rejected the type on the flimsy ground that its landing speed of 49 m.p.h. (78·8 km/hr.) was too high for the small French airfields. Only one hundred and twenty-five M.1Cs were ordered, and probably fewer than twenty of these saw operational service, none of them on the Western Front. They formed the partial equipment of No. 72 Squadron in Mesopotamia and Nos. 17, 47 and 150 Squadrons in Macedonia. In this theatre, where the main need was for a good escort fighter, the short range of the M.1C limited its usefulness. The remaining M.1Cs were allocated to training units in the United Kingdom and Egypt. By 31 October 1918 the R.A.F. had only forty-seven M.1Cs on charge, thirty-one of these at home stations. The M.1C had the 110 h.p. Le Rhône, cut-outs in both wing roots and the machine-gun mounted centrally.

Six M.1Cs were given to Chile in 1917, one making the first aerial crossing of the Andes on 12 December 1918. Four were repurchased by Bristol after the Armistice, two of which later went to Spain and the United States. Another aircraft, redesignated M.1D after being re-

engined with a 100 h.p. Bristol Lucifer engine, became the civil G-EAVP. This aircraft won races at Croydon in 1922, but was lost in a crash in 1923. One M.1C was flown out to Australia, where, in much-modified form as VH-UQI with a de Havilland Gipsy engine, it won the 1932 Australian Aerial Derby.

68 Thulin designs (various)

In seven years before his untimely death in 1919 Dr. Enoch Thulin probably did more than any other man to lay the foundations of a Swedish aviation industry. In 1913, with Oskar Ask, he founded the Aeroplanvarvet i Skåne (AVIS) and built two Blériot-type monoplanes with 50 h.p. Gnome engines. In the following year Thulin and some other associates of his took over the AVIS company completely, renaming it AB Enoch Thulins Aeroplanfabrik (AETA); the new company's first products were a further twenty-three of the Blériot-type machines. Two of these were delivered to the Swedish Army Aviation Service, and the remainder were used at the Flight School at Ljungbyhed, also run by Dr. Thulin. These aircraft were designated Thulin Type A; the Thulin B, eight of which were built between 1915 and 1917, was a copy of a 2-seat Morane-Saulnier monoplane. Four of these were used at Thulin's flying school, two others were sold to the Swedish Navy and the other pair to the Danish Army. The Thulin C was an Albatros B.II, an example of which was interned in Sweden in 1914, and he Thulin D was a Morane-Saulnier parasol monoplane copy, five of which were completed, two of them for the Swedish Army. Two others went to Finland in March 1918, where they took part in the Finnish 'war of liberation and national independence'. Of four or more Thulin Type Es built, the Swedish Army received two, and also eight Thulin FAs; both of these were 2-seat reconnaissance aircraft. Two other Type FAs were sold to Holland. The Navy accepted five Thulin G and two GA floatplane 2-seaters, powered by 150 h.p. Benz and 200 h.p. Curtiss engines respectively.

One of the Swedish engineer's most interesting designs was the Type H, the sole example of which was first flown in 1917. This was the world's first three-engined float-plane, and was driven by three 90 h.p. Thulin A (Gnome copy) rotary engines. The Type H was later flown as a landplane; it was ordered by the Army, but although successful it was cancelled in 1918. The design built in the greatest numbers was the Type K, the subject of the illustration. This was a single-seat fighter design, first produced in 1917, and eighteen aircraft of this type were eventually completed. The first two machines were delivered to the Royal Swedish Army Aviation as aircraft Nos. 21 and 23; one was owned privately by Dr. Thulin and fifteen were sold in 1917–19 to the Royal Netherlands Naval Air Service. The Thulin Type K, a stocky little machine bearing obvious traces of its Blériot/Morane ancestry, was never used as

a fighter, and there is no record that a gun was ever fitted.

Another type to enter both Swedish and Dutch Army service was the Type L and its derivative the LA, five and fifteen respectively being built between 1916 and 1918. The Type N, flown for the first time on 30 December 1917 with a 135 h.p. Thulin G rotary engine, was an experimental single-seat fighter. From it was developed (with the same engine) the Type NA flown in 1921. During the six years of its existence the AETA company built altogether ninety-nine aircraft, peak output being in 1918 when thirty-two were produced. After Dr. Thulin's death in a flying accident in 1919 a new factory, the AB Thulin-verken, was founded in 1920. It is still in existence at the present day, but has no connection with aviation.

69 Fokker E types

The air supremacy enjoyed by the Fokker monoplane fighters over the Western Front must have been more than usually galling to the French in particular, for the Fokker E types' design was influenced by the Morane-Saulnier Type H monoplane, and they carried an interrupter gear developed by Fokker's engineers after capturing Roland Garros' Morane-Saulnier Type L.

The Fokker M.5 which gave rise to the E types was first flown in 1913. From it were developed the long-span M.5L and the short-span M.5K. Both were powered by the 80 h.p. Oberursel rotary and used in modest numbers early in the war;

a few M.5Ls served with the Austro-Hungarian air arm. Following the capture of Garros' Morane L in April 1915, Fokker engineers developed an interrupter gear that was tested on an M.5K. Two other M.5Ks were similarly tested using a Spandau gun, and this version went into urgent production as the E.I; front-line units began to score mounting successes as their E.Is were delivered from June 1915, and production is believed to have totalled sixty-eight. The E.I, essentially a 'rush job', was quickly followed by the E.II in which the 100 h.p. Oberursel was installed. Other E.II modifications included a reduction in wing size, which made it more difficult to fly without any appreciable increase in performance. Deliveries, of about fifty E.IIs, began in July 1915.

The most numerous version was the E.III, with wings extended to a span greater than the original E.I. The E.III was normally fitted with a single 7·92 mm. Spandau gun; a few were flown with twin guns, but the extra weight imposed an unacceptable penalty on performance. Two hundred and sixty E.IIIs are thought to have been completed, being used by the German Army and the Austro-Hungarian Air Service, which had also received a few E.Is. An attempt to produce a viable two-gun fighter resulted in the E.IV, whose prototype appeared in November 1915. This was given a 160 h.p. two-row Oberursel, and the wings were further extended to 32 ft. 9⅔ in. (10·00 m.). However, the E.IV, although faster than the

E.III, proved to be much less manoeuvrable, and only about forty-five were built. For a brief period Max Immelmann flew a three-gun E.IV but he later reverted to a standard two-gun machine. In E types serving with the Austro-Hungarian forces the domestic 8 mm. Schwarzlose gun was usually substituted for the German weapon.

The Fokker E types were in service on the Western Front from mid-1915 until late summer 1916. Their peak period of effectiveness began about October, and from then until January they reigned virtually unopposed in European skies. This lack of opposition led to the almost legendary success of the 'Fokker scourge', which was out of all proportion to the actual numbers in service. Their chief victim was the luckless B.E.2c, which soon earned a reputation as 'Fokker fodder'. From January 1916 the Fokkers began to encounter worthier opposition in the form of the D.H.2, Nieuport 11 and F.E.2b, which had virtually dispelled the Fokker's menace by the spring. The E types continued until the end of 1916 on the Eastern Front and in Mesopotamia, Palestine and Turkey, but thereafter were used almost exclusively for training.

70 Junkers D.I

The evolution by Dr. Hugo Junkers of all-metal monoplanes with cantilever wings began in 1915, the first to be built being the J.1, which flew for the first time on 12 December that year. (This should not be confused with the military J.I, which was a 2-seat biplane and had the factory designation J.4) A number of other monoplane prototypes followed, but the true precursor of the D.I fighter was the J.7 of October 1917. This appeared in at least three forms, but whether these were separate machines or successive modifications to the first is uncertain. The J.7 was powered by a 160 h.p. Mercedes D.III, whose radiator was mounted, as if as an afterthought, on top of the cylinder block: a frontal radiator was fitted later. A novel feature was the use of pivoting wing-tips instead of conventional ailerons, but these were found to create wing flutter and were later replaced by ailerons.

The direct prototype of the D.I was the J.9, which appeared in March 1918 and was basically a refined J.7 with slightly bigger dimensions. Accounts of the production and service record of the D.I are conflicting. The machine that took part in the second D types competition at Adlershof in May/June 1918 was described as a J.9, and at that time was powered by a Mercedes D.IIIa of 180 h.p. In a list of types evaluated by leading German pilots in July, the only Junkers product was referred to as a D.I and had a standard Mercedes D.III: this seems to imply that the first production order was placed at about this time. The powerplant intended for production Junkers D.Is is believed to have been the 185 h.p. B.M.W. IIIa, and a D.I with this engine took part in the third D types competition in October 1918; but it is thought that the 160 h.p. Mercedes powered at least some

of the early production aircraft. Many authorities refer to a total of forty-one D.Is at the Front when the Armistice was signed, but it seems more likely that this figure represented the number of machines actually built at that time, with only a comparative handful having reached front-line *Jastas*; some notice would surely have been taken of larger quantities of such a fast and manoeuvrable fighter, especially one of such distinctive appearance, in the closing stages of the war. This supposition is strengthened by reports that the D.I's flying qualities were unsatisfactory in some respects. An alternative explanation may be that early production aircraft delivered with Mercedes D.IIIs were recalled later for refitting with more powerful B.M.Ws. At least one D.I had a Vee-type in-line engine: this could have been the Daimler D.IIIb, which had a similar output to the B.M.W. IIIa. The D.I was armed with twin forward-firing synchronised Spandau machine-guns and with the B.M.W. engine could climb to 5,000 m. (16,404 ft.) in 22¼ minutes.

71 Junkers CL.I

The CL.I was a 2-seater escort/ground-attack derivative of the D.I fighter. The prototype, which bore the factory designation J.10, had overhung horn-balanced ailerons and was powered by a 160 h.p. Mercedes D.III. It flew for the first time on 4 May 1918. Production of the CL.I started in the summer, and forty-seven had been delivered by the end of the war; not all of these are thought to have reached the Front. They had shorter-span, plain ailerons and 180 h.p. Mercedes D.IIIa engines. Armament consisted of two 7·92 mm. forward-firing Spandau machine-guns in front of the pilot and a single Parabellum on an elevated ring mounting in the observer's cockpit. Racks were situated on each side of the fuselage, abreast of the rear cockpit, in which stick grenades or other anti-personnel weapons could be carried when the CL.I was used for ground attack. The Junkers CL.I was probably the best ground-attack type produced in Germany during the war, but it arrived at the Front too late to make any impact. It was fast, manoeuvrable and very strongly built, and could climb to 3,000 m. (9,843 ft.) in 14 minutes. The type did see some post-war combat service in Finland and one or two Baltic states, and at least one machine was used in a civil capacity. This was fitted with a canopy over the rear seat and used on a commercial basis by Junkers in 1919– in all probability the first all-metal aircraft ever to operate an air service. It may have been the same aircraft that later became D-78 on the German civil register.

Three examples were built late in 1918 of a twin-float variant, the CLS.I. The substitution of floats increased the overall length to 29 ft. 4⅓ in. (8·95 m.), the additional side area being compensated by the addition of a small, triangular fixed fin; span was increased by 2 ft. 3½ in. (0·70 m.). Despite its greater all-up weight, the CLS.I, powered by a

195 h.p. Bz.IIIb, had a better level speed – 180 km/hr. (111·8 m.p.h.) – than the landplane. However, some troubles were encountered with the tail design and the CLS.I did not go into production.

72 Hansa-Brandenburg CC

The first Brandenburg flying boat was the 3-seat FB developed by Ernst Heinkel from a Lohner design and built in small numbers for the German and Austro-Hungarian Navies in 1915. In 1916 Heinkel produced an original design for a single-seat wooden-hulled fighter flying boat, which he named CC after Camillo Castiglioni, financial controller of the Brandenburg company. The CC was characterised by 'star-strut' interplane bracing like that used for the D.I landplane fighter. After flight trials with the prototype a single CC was ordered by the German Navy. This was delivered to Warnemünde in February 1917, powered by a 150 h.p. Bz.III engine and armed with a centrally mounted Spandau front gun. Two CC production batches totalling thirty-five aircraft were delivered during 1917; these had wing radiators and a twin-Spandau armament. Some also had slightly lengthened hulls.

Major user of the CC was the Austro-Hungarian Navy, for whom the type was built by Phönix. Designated in the A class in Austrian service, the flying boats were used up and down the Adriatic in defence of ports and naval bases. Like their German counterparts, they were at first fitted with one, and later with two, machine-guns; it may be supposed that these were the domestic 8 mm. Schwarzlose weapon. The CC's chief opponent in the Adriatic was the Italian Air Force's Nieuport 11, against which the flying boats acquitted themselves fairly well, having a slight edge in speed to offset their lesser manoeuvrability. Overall Phönix production of the CC amounted to thirty-five aircraft (A.13–42 and A.45–49). Machine A45 appeared in 1918 as a triplane, but this line of development was not pursued. The 'Phönix A' designation was also applied to sixty-one examples of the Hansa-Brandenburg W.18 seaplane built for the Austro-Hungarian Navy. Examples of the CC in German service included at least one aircraft with a spinner and the engine in a streamlined, egg-shaped nacelle, and another with extra V-struts outboard of the 'star' struts.

73 Macchi L.1 and L.2, M.3 to M.12

Macchi's association with waterborne aircraft began almost by accident. In May 1915 the Austrian Lohner flying boat L40 fell into Italian hands, and was delivered to S.A. Nieuport-Macchi with the request that a copy be produced for the Italian Navy. Designated L.1 to signify its Lohner origin, the first example was completed by June 1915. It was similar to the Austrian design except for its 150 h.p. Isotta-Fraschini engine and forward-firing Revelli machine-gun. One hundred and thirty-nine L.1s were built, serving from late 1915

until autumn 1916, when they were replaced by F.B.A. flying boats. A lighter development, the L.2, with a 160 h.p. Isotta-Fraschini V-4B, had a much better performance, but only ten were completed. Further development introduced so many new features that the L.3 could justifiably be regarded as a Macchi design, and it was renamed M.3 on its adoption by the Italian Navy. One M.3 established a height record of 5,400 m. (17,716·5 ft.) in 1916; and just over two hundred M.3s were built for the *Regia Marina Italiana*. These were employed throughout the Adriatic on reconnaissance, bombing, escort and ground support. In the bombing role they carried four 110 kg. bombs.

Macchi's first flying boat fighter was the M.5, designed by Buzio and Calzavara. This was a single-seater (the earlier types having been 2/3-seaters), with two 6·5 mm. Revelli machine-guns in the nose. Usual powerplant was the V-4B, though some later aircraft had the 250 h.p. V-6B. Two hundred and forty M.5s were built, being delivered to the 260a, 261a, 286a, 287a and 288a *Squadriglie della Marina* from early 1918 and serving until the Armistice. The M.5 was extremely manoeuvrable, had sufficient range to perform escort duty and could climb to 4,000 m. (13,123 ft.) in 20 minutes.

However, it was not quite fast enough to compete with the Austrian Navy's Phönix D.I, and Macchi developed the M.7, powered by the V-6B engine, to match or exceed the speed of the Phönix. In this they were successful, for the smaller M.7, despite a higher gross weight, was faster and better than its predecessor, and could climb to 5,000 m. (16,404 ft.) in 22 minutes. Unfortunately, of two hundred ordered only seventeen were delivered by the Armistice and only three had become operational. Production continued after the war, but it has not been established whether the full two hundred were completed. In 1919–20 the Royal Swedish Army Aviation purchased three M.7s. Post-war variants included the M.7bis (one of which won the 1921 Schneider Trophy), M.7ter AR and M.7terB. The latest versions, with 475 h.p. Lorraine engines, were still in service in 1923.

A patrol development of the M.3 appeared late in 1917 as the 2-seat M.8. This retained the V-4B powerplant in a bigger and stronger airframe, and was armed with a movable gun in the prow. It carried a similar warload to the M.3, plus photographic and radio equipment. Fifty-seven were built by the Armistice, primarily for coastal patrol and anti-shipping duties. They remained in service post-war as trainers. One M.8 was presented in 1919 to the Royal Swedish Naval Aviation, this aircraft having a 180 h.p. Franco-Tosi Lagnano engine. The M.9 was an enlarged development with a 300 h.p. Fiat A-12bis engine. Plans were made in 1918 to build several hundred, but only thirty were completed, and only sixteen delivered, by the Armistice. They remained in service until the mid-

1920s. Another wartime model was the M.12, a 3-seat development of the M.9 with a 450 h.p. Ansaldo-San Giorgio 4E 28 engine. This had fore and aft gun positions, connected by a tunnel in the fuselage so that they could be manned by one gunner. The M.12's broad front hull and twin tailbooms afforded the rear gun an excellent field of fire. Like the M.9, the M.12 was too late for war service, but a few were delivered to the Italian Navy; they figured in trans-Mediterranean flights and Schneider events in later years. Demilitarised versions used commercially after the war included M.3s in service with a Swiss operator and the M.9bis and M.9ter.

74 Albatros W.4
The German Admiralty, disturbed by attacks on its seaplane bases along the Flanders coast, issued a specification in the summer of 1916 for a single-seat station defence fighter. The simplest way to meet this quickly was to adapt an existing design, and the Albatros Werke accordingly produced a seaplane fighter based on the D.I landplane. The new fighter, designated W.4, utilised a number of D.I components but had a much larger gap between the fuselage and upper wings, which were of 1 m. (3 ft. 3⅜ in.) greater span; the underfin of the D.I was eliminated, the normal fin and tailplane being increased correspondingly in size, and the aircraft was mounted on twin, square-section floats.

In September 1916 the first W.4 (747) was delivered to the German

Navy. A second machine followed later that month, and a third in December. Powerplant was the well-tried Mercedes D.III in-line, and the fighter was armed with a pair of 7·92 mm. Spandau machine-guns on top of the fuselage, firing on either side of the cylinder block. Between February and April 1917 the first ten production W.4s were delivered. These had better streamlined floats with revised strutting, and a smaller cockpit. Further batches of twenty, ten, twenty-five, thirty and twenty W.4s brought the total to one hundred and eighteen by December 1917. Some later batches had a wing radiator offset to starboard instead of Windhoff side radiators, and were fitted with ailerons on all four wings. A variety of different float designs were used.

The W.4s served principally along the Flanders coast, but some were also reported in action in the Aegean area. By the time the final production batches were being delivered, the W.4 – essentially an interim fighter – was being replaced by the equally fast but better defended Hansa-Brandenburg W.12 2-seater. The W.4 possessed a first-class endurance, good speed, manoeuvrability and firepower, and gave a good account of itself during its brief operational life against Allied floatplanes, but it found the later R.N.A.S. flying boats somewhat tougher opposition. It could climb to 1,000 m. (3,280 ft.) in 5 minutes.

75 Rumpler 6B

The urgent need by the German Navy during the last two years of war for water-borne fighters to defend its seaplane bases and neighbouring coastal areas was met by three principal aircraft types, all adaptations of existing landplanes. The Albatros W.4 and Brandenburg KDW were evolved from their manufacturers' respective D.I fighters; Rumpler had no single-seat fighter of its own, and so the Type 6B floatplane was based on its 2-seat C.I reconnaissance aircraft. It therefore needed more modification than the other designs, and this took the form of forward stagger for the wings, the elimination of the second cockpit and the fitting of a large plain rudder to offset the additional side area of the twin-step floats. The elevators and triangular tailplane were reduced slightly in area on production 6Bs.

The initial version was the 6B-1, first examples of which were delivered in July 1916. By the end of the year about a dozen were in service, and thirty-eight had been delivered by the end of May 1917. They served mainly with the German seaplane centres at Zeebrugge and Ostend; some were employed in the Black Sea area to defend German bases from attacks by Russian flying boats. From October 1917 a new version, the Rumpler 6B-2, began to join the 6B-1 in service. These retained the same powerplant, but their airframes were based on the Rumpler C.IV landplane, with bigger dimensions and a 'wing-nut' horizontal tail. Despite a poorer performance, fifty 6B-2s were ordered, delivery taking place between October 1917 and January 1918. For some reason one aircraft was not delivered and its place was taken by an 'extra' 6B-1 delivered in January 1918. Both versions were armed with a synchronised 7·92 mm. Spandau front gun mounted on the port side of the engine block.

76 Hansa-Brandenburg KDW

The abbreviation KDW, standing for *Kampf Doppeldecker, Wasser* (Fighting Biplane, Water), was a general type classification and not the military designation of any one specific aeroplane: the Hansa-Brandenburg CC flying boat, which was also a single-seat fighter, is often referred to as a KDW. However, the description is generally understood to apply to the W.9 floatplane fighter evolved by Ernst Heinkel in mid-1916. This was basically an adaptation of the landplane D.I 'starstrutter'. Apart from substituting floats for the wheeled landing gear, other alterations included adding a small underfin and increasing the wing span. View from the cockpit was improved by enlarging the cutout in the top wing and by leaving small cut-outs in the lower-wing roots; the engine mounting was also revised to give a better view forward.

The KDW was brought into being to supplement the Albatros W.4 and Rumpler 6B as a defensive fighter to protect seaplane bases on the Flanders and Adriatic coasts. It is some indication of the KDW's value,

and of the priority afforded to German Naval aircraft in general, that the first aircraft was completed in September 1916 and the fifty-eighth was not delivered until February 1918. It is hardly surprising that by the time all KDWs had been delivered they were outdated, and had already begun to be replaced by later types with better performance and greater versatility. The KDWs were built in five batches. The first three aircraft had 150 h.p. Bz.III engines; the next ten, powered by 160 h.p. Mercedes D.IIIs, had flush-mounted wing radiators that became standard on subsequent aircraft. The third batch, also of ten aircraft, reverted to the Bz.III, but had smaller rudders. The fourth and fifth batches, of fifteen and twenty respectively, were powered by 160 h.p. Maybach Mb.IIIs, had shorter floats, a shallow dorsal fin and a non-balanced rudder. On all except the final batch, armament comprised a single fixed Spandau gun on the port side of the engine block and – like those of the D.I landplane – still out of reach of the pilot. Only on the last twenty aircraft, which had twin Spandaus, were the guns moved back to a position within reach from the cockpit.

Variants of the KDW included the W.11, three of which were built with 200 h.p. Bz.IV engines and increased wing span; the W.16 (one built) with a 160 h.p. U.III rotary engine; and the W.25 (one built), which was similar to the Bz.III-engined KDW, but had orthodox wing bracing.

77 Hansa-Brandenburg W.12 and W.19

The Imperial German Navy learned from experience that single-seat seaplanes were vulnerable to attack from the rear, and so in the autumn of 1916 Ernst Heinkel began to design the 2-seat W.12. The prototype was completed in January 1917. Its fuselage maintained an almost even depth from nose to tail, giving plenty of 'keel' to make the W.12 stable in flight without affecting its manoeuvrability. The tailplane was mounted on top of the fuselage, with a balanced, comma-type rudder extending behind and below the sternpost. Hence, from the elevated gunring in the rear cockpit, the observer commanded a virtually uninterrupted field of fire in the upper hemisphere.

Despite an accident to the prototype, the W.12 was ordered into production, one hundred and forty-five being delivered between April 1917 and March 1918. These were in batches as follows: six with 160 h.p. Mercedes D.IIIs and wing radiators; four batches of nine, twenty, twenty and thirty with 150 h.p. Bz.IIIs and frontal radiators, and two final batches of forty and twenty Mercedes-engined W.12s. Minor variations occurred between different batches. The fourth Benz-powered batch had twin forward-firing Spandaus, the remainder a single one to starboard; all W.12s had a Parabellum gun in the rear cockpit. The W.12 entered service in April 1917, and as well as giving an excellent account of itself defending German seaplane and naval bases against Allied aeroplanes and airships, it was often used for reconnaissance.

From November 1917 it was joined in production by the W.19, fifty-four of which were built, entering service from January 1918. The W.19 had blunter wings, 2·60 m. (8 ft. 6⅓ in.) greater in span; a 1·05 m. (3 ft. 5⅓ in.) longer fuselage; revised tail surfaces; and a 240 h.p. Maybach Mb.IV engine. All except the first three had twin Spandau guns, and one was fitted experimentally with a 20 mm. Becker cannon in the observer's cockpit. The W.19 had an endurance of 5 hours, and often worked in company with the W.12, patrolling ahead of its smaller companion and returning to fetch it when a target was sighted. The Brandenburg 2-seaters, used in some concentration during spring and summer 1918, were treated by R.N.A.S. crews along the Flanders coast and over the North Sea as adversaries worthy of respect. Both types remained in service until the Armistice.

The W.27 was a variant with a 195 h.p. Bz.IIIb; it remained a prototype only, but two similar W.32s were completed with Mercedes D.IIIs and used as trainers.

78 Curtiss N-9

In spite of the fact that it was a standard primary trainer of the U.S. Navy for close on ten years, the Curtiss N-9 remains an almost forgotten member of the 'Jenny' family. It first appeared at the end of 1916, when the U.S. Navy was seeking to expand its pilot-training programme quickly and issued its requirements for a school aircraft to the home industry. Curtiss, having already evolved the JN landplane trainer, were able to produce such a machine more easily than rival manufacturers.

The basis for the N-9 was the JN-4B, a long-span version of the JN-4A; this had been rejected by the Signal Corps, but its greater wing area was well suited to compensate for the additional weight and area of a float undercarriage. Thus the prototype N-9 was basically the 'Jenny' with wings 10 ft. (3·05 m.) greater in span by increasing the size of the centre-sections, and with a 100 h.p. Curtiss OXX-6 engine, a slightly uprated version of the landplane's OX-5.

Production orders for both the Army and Navy had already been placed before America's entry into the war in April 1917, and the Navy orders were soon substantially increased, to a point where Curtiss were unable to handle the entire production. One hundred and thirty-six Naval serial numbers were allotted for Curtiss-built N-9s, of which only a hundred were actually completed. The bulk of N-9 production was carried out by the Burgess Co., who built three hundred and sixty of these aircraft; contracts for a further one thousand two hundred were cancelled after the Armistice.

Delivery of N-9s began to the U.S. Naval Training School at Pensacola and other Army and Navy training establishments early in 1917. The U.S. Army used fourteen N-9s, an earlier order for six aircraft having been transferred to the Navy. Once in service, it was found that the OXX-6 engine, despite its extra power, gave the N-9 a poorer performance than the OX-5-engined JN-4s; as a result, many of the floatplanes were re-engined or built from scratch with 150 h.p. Wright-built Hispano-Suiza engines, with which they were designated N-9H. The 'Hisso' installation was characterised by a blunter nose, with a shallow, bowl-shaped spinner, and a tall vertical radiator on top of the fuselage behind the cylinder block.

Replacement of the N-9s in U.S. Navy service began in 1924, and the type was finally withdrawn in 1927. In the early 1920s a further fifty trainers were assembled at the Pensacola Naval Air Station from spares and salvaged components. One of the Burgess N-9s was modified into the short-span N-10, but this version did not go into production.

79 Sablatnig floatplanes

Dr. Josef Sablatnig, an Austrian by birth, built an aeroplane as early as 1903. Moving to Germany, he acquired German nationality and formed the Sablatnig Flugzeugbau in October 1915. In the same month the first Sablatnig-designed seaplane appeared. This was the unarmed SF1, a twin-float biplane with a 160 h.p. Mercedes engine. After it had been tested by the German Navy a modified version was ordered as the SF2, whose prototype differed chiefly in having redesigned vertical tail surfaces. These were revised still further on production SF2s, twenty-six of which were built – six by the parent company, and ten each by L.F.G. and L.V.G. Delivery took place between June 1916 and May 1917, and they were used chiefly as trainers for Navy pilots. The SF3 was a heavier, scaled-up development or the SF2 intended as an escort and patrol aircraft. It was powered by a 220 h.p. Benz Bz.IV and had a ring-mounted Parabellum gun in the observer's cockpit. The sole SF3 was tested in autumn 1917.

The next 2-seat development was the SF5, basically an improved SF2. The SF5 had a 150 h.p. Bz.III; ninety-one were built, fifty by Sablatnig as reconnaissance and coastal patrol aircraft with radio equipment and an observer's gun. It is reported that their performance was poor and they were not a great success. They appeared over the North Sea and the Baltic, and in the latter theatre particularly suffered at the hands of Russian Nieuport fighters. The remaining SF5s (ten by L.F.G., thirty by L.V.G. and one 'straggler' from Sablatnig) were delivered as trainers without guns or radio, and it is likely that some of the earlier SF5s were recalled and reallocated to training establishments. Delivery took place between January 1917 and February 1918. One SF5 was converted experimentally to a wheeled undercarriage with the designation SF6. Three examples were ordered of the SF7, a 2-seat fighter development of the SF3. Only one was completed, being delivered in September 1917. It was powered by a 240 h.p. Maybach Mb.IV and had

a forward-firing Spandau in addition to the Parabellum gun. Its performance was no more than average.

The final Sablatnig design to be built was the SF8. This was evolved expressly as a trainer, reverting to the Bz.III engine and having dual cockpit controls and no armament. Delivery began in spring 1918 of orders totalling thirty-three SF8s, but it is uncertain whether all of these were completed.

One single-seat Sablatnig aircraft was also built. This was the SF4, basically a scaled-down version of the SF2 intended for the seaplane station defence role. It was powered by a Bz.III and had a single forward-firing Spandau gun. Two prototypes were completed during the early months of 1917, one as a sesquiplane, the other as a triplane, but neither was very successful.

80 Hansa-Brandenburg W.29 and W.33

It has been suggested that Oberleutnant Christiansen, commander of the important German Naval air base at Zeebrugge, played a part in urging the development of the W.29: certainly he was invited to fly the prototype, and he may have been allowed to take it back with him to Zeebrugge in February 1918 for operational use. Heinkel's development of the W.29 took the logical form of a monoplane version of the successful W.12, retaining the Benz engine in a shorter but basically similar fuselage. The slightly tapered single wings were increased in span and chord to give a total area almost equal to that of the biplane, and the tailplane was also altered slightly.

The first W.29 model to be built could really be regarded as a fighter, being a fast and very manoeuvrable aircraft with twin forward-firing guns and a Parabellum gun in the rear cockpit. It was powered by a 195 h.p. Bz. IIIb. The first six W.29s were to this pattern, as were a further four ordered later in 1918, although there is some doubt whether this second batch was completed. Between these two orders came four other batches totalling seventy aircraft. The first twenty had the standard Bz.III, and radio equipment instead of one of the front guns. A second similar batch of twenty may not all have been delivered. The remaining thirty W.29s, with Bz. IIIs, had two front guns and no radio. Three W.29s were built by Ufag before the Armistice, for the Austro-Hungarian Navy, but were not delivered. The W.29 entered German Naval service from about April 1918, serving alongside the W.12 and W.19 and often undertaking combined missions with the W.19. Like the earlier Brandenburgs, they were treated with healthy respect by Allied sub-marines, surface vessels, flying boats and airships. Most of their successes were achieved by concentrated fire-power, but some W.29s carried a small bomb load. In mid-1918 a still larger version, the W.33, appeared; this had a 15·85 m. (52 ft. 0 in.) wing span. Twenty-six were apparently ordered, but it seems that only six were completed before the Armistice. The first three had two front guns and 260 h.p. Maybach engines; the next two had single front guns and 300 h.p. Basse und Selve engines, but were later refitted with Maybachs. The last of the six (presumably Maybach-powered) had one front gun and a 20 mm. Becker cannon in the rear cockpit. A later and still larger version, the W.34 (300 h.p. Fiat), was too late for war service, but some were purchased by the Finnish and Latvian Air Forces after the war. Some W.33s and W.29s were also acquired post-war by the Finnish and Royal Danish Air Forces respectively. Not only were the Brandenburg monoplane floatplanes first-class combat machines in themselves, but their general characteristics were also reflected in a number of prototypes from other manufacturers late in 1918.

APPENDIX 1

THE research into the aircraft colour schemes illustrated in this volume is the work of Ian D. Huntley, A.M.R.Ae.S., whose studies of aircraft colours and markings have been made over a period of more than twenty years. Ian Huntley was one of a small team of experts formed from members of the Royal Aeronautical Society and the Society of Licensed Aircraft Engineers in 1958 to undertake full-scale restoration work on the aircraft of the Nash Collection, which was bought by the R.Ae.S. in December 1953. With the title Historic Aircraft Maintenance Group, this body began work at Hendon, transferring its activities later to the B.E.A. Engineering Base at London (Heathrow) Airport. After 1 April 1964 the aircraft were gradually dispersed to various R.A.F. stations in the United Kingdom for continued restoration and are now on permanent loan to the Royal Air Force Museum at Hendon for display. Effectively, this meant that the official duties of the H.A.M.G. ceased towards the end of 1965, but Ian Huntley and A. S. Hughes, the H.A.M.G.'s Chief Engineer, continue to act as civilian consultants on the subject of historic aircraft restoration.

Soon after the move to Heathrow an appeal was made for information that would contribute towards restoring the various aircraft in authentic colour schemes, and a landslide of 'bits and pieces' arrived in response. In August 1961 a second similar appeal brought a second similar flood of information and material. Inevitably, much of it was too vague or contradictory, and the only satisfactory way to solve the problems and establish the true colour finishes was to trace the original paint specifications and to approach manufacturers to re-create paints and materials from them. Ian Huntley became a 'one-man Specifications Committee' charged with this task and with classifying and authenticating the material submitted. As a result he was in a unique position to advise on the completion of the colour illustrations in this volume, and the real hues of many colours can now be seen for the first time since World War 1.

Such research proves, if proof is needed, that the only really satisfactory method of recording and relaying colour information must be based on first-hand inspection of the colours concerned, whether *in situ* on present-day aircraft or in the form of re-created samples; these must then be related to a comprehensive dictionary of colours which gives a key 'code' for individual shades of a given colour. This is the formula adopted in preparing the illustrations in this series, for which we use as our main colour dictionary *The Methuen Handbook of Colour* by A. Kornerup and J. H. Wanscher.* This handbook gives a spectrum of colour variations that are especially well related to aircraft paint finishes through the years, and when correct colour values, using this handbook to code them, are compared with most existing verbal or pictorial representations of specific aircraft types, the need for a standardised scheme of reporting and portraying colour values is self-evident; and the inadequacy of mere verbal descriptions, such as 'dark green' or 'pale blue', is also woefully apparent – there are dozens of them. The need to have a standard system is especially urgent in the case of aircraft of the 1914–18 period, where the number of people with first-hand knowledge of these aircraft is diminishing rapidly.

There is still, unfortunately, an almost unbelievable lack even of good basic general knowledge about aircraft colour finishes – something like *eighty-five per cent* of the material submitted to the H.A.M.G. was either the result of guesswork or the perpetuation of a long-standing fallacy. Much of the guesswork undoubtedly arises from the fact that most photographs taken during the war and reproduced then or since were taken on film which was not colour-sensitive and which in any case gave only a black and white result. A little orthochromatic, and even less panchromatic, film was then available which, with appropriate colour filters, could give a more accurate tonal rendering of colours within the limits of a black and white medium. Uncertainty regarding the type of film used to take a particular photograph is therefore a contributory factor: one type, for example, may make a red rudder stripe appear darker than a blue one, while another type will give the

* First published by Politikens Forlag, Copenhagen, in 1961, and by Methuen & Co., London, in 1963 (revised 1967).

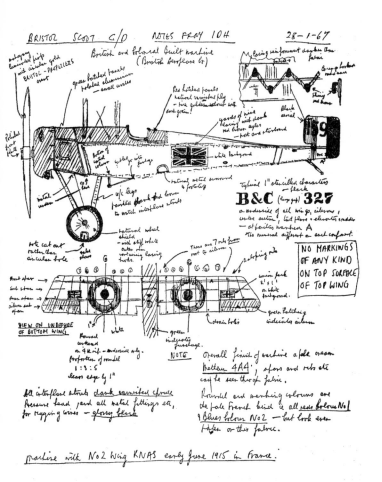

Typical sketch produced by Ian Huntley as a basic guide for artists preparing the colour plates in this series.

reverse effect. All too often an inaccuracy arises, probably quite innocently, from an incorrect deduction made from such evidence; and 'for want of a nail' the error gradually gathers weight as more and more followers accept it and repeat it until it attains the status of an unassailable fact. There is not the space here to discuss individual cases at length, but one of the commonest misconceptions, which concerns the British P.C.10 khaki finish of World War 1, is dealt with in some detail in Appendix 2.

World War 1 was as much a forcing ground for the evolution of aircraft protective finishes – in all senses – as it was for the design of the machines themselves, and German and Italian aircraft, many of which had ply-covered fuselages, were able from a comparatively early date to employ disruptive camouflage schemes. Britain lagged somewhat behind the other powers in this technique, but by the time of the Armistice improvisation had been overtaken by a more serious study of the art of camouflage. In this respect the Salamander represents an interesting outcome of one such study. Up to 1917 use was made only of doping schemes that employed a first coating of clear shrinking dope, followed by a protective covering of pigmented varnish medium (a cellulose material with a similar base to clear dope but with its shrinking powers counteracted by the addition of a proportion of castor oil). During 1917, however, experiments showed that a pigmented dope not only gave an ideal fabric finish but saved time and eliminated the need to use such large quantities of cellulose material. From this it was established that, by using the ideal tropical sun-resisting pigment in the dope – P.C.12, a dark reddish-brown (as illustrated on pages 18 and 83) – almost any finishing colour could be applied on top, all within the normal five coats, and yet maximum fabric protection was still maintained. This eventually led to the introduction of dark red-brown priming dope for use on fabric, a practice which is still in use today. Speculation naturally arose whether colours other than the standard dark brown could be used that would have a more concealing effect, and in summer 1918 various combinations of colour and pattern were studied to decide between 'dazzle' or 'splinter' schemes using bright and contrasting colours, and 'concealing' schemes made up of gently curving areas painted in dull, blending colours. Tests were carried out using various 'dummy' wings and, subsequently, B.E.2c, Camel, F.K.3 and Salamander aircraft for actual flight trials.

The four matt colours used in the Salamander scheme were advertised in later years by Cellon Ltd. as 'Salamander colours', and several contractors building British observation aircraft were asked to prepare drawings showing the aircraft in these colours.

Other traps for the unwary exist when dealing with the 'lozenge' finishes adopted by the German and Austro-Hungarian air services. For one thing, there were probably more distinct patterns and colour combinations in printed schemes than is usually appreciated, quite apart from hand-painted schemes applied extempore by units in the field. The shapes of the 'lozenges' themselves varied from regular hexagons to irregular polygons, and generally a second fabric, of similar pattern but lighter tones, would be used for the undersides of the wings and horizontal tail surfaces. In one scheme, for example, the upper-surface and fuselage colours were Prussian blue, blue-green, dark ochre, sage green and dark violet; corresponding colours on the undersides were pink, blue, ochre, pale green and pale violet. Some lozenge fabrics were printed in as many as six or seven separate colours.

The error most commonly made, however, is in the incorrect *application* of a given scheme to an illustration or model, rather than the use of an inaccurate pattern. Thus, while the actual basic pattern may be quite correct, the *effect* is incorrect because it has been applied in the wrong direction. So far as the printed lozenge fabrics are concerned – obviously no hard and fast rules can be laid down for hand-painted schemes – the first stage was to evolve a unit pattern outline, and there were at least three of these in common use. This would then be engraved on rollers to print longitudinally on a standard roll of unbleached linen fabric so that the pattern was repeated along the length of the roll. Since the fabric was naturally much stronger across its width than along its length, the standard practice was to apply it chordwise to the flying surfaces – i.e. with the short fibres parallel to the wing main spar(s), the pattern repeating from leading edge to trailing edge or vice versa, and not spanwise from wing root to wingtip as is often supposed. The fabric, usually from 4–4½ ft. wide, was normally applied beginning at the centre-line of the upper wings or the roots of the lower wings and working outward towards the tips. This could vary on individual types, for example to avoid a seam between two strips of fabric coming in the way of an aileron control wire. Many German aircraft, mostly the larger types, had their wing fabric applied at 45 degrees to the leading edge, whereas British practice was to discourage this arrangement during the war period.

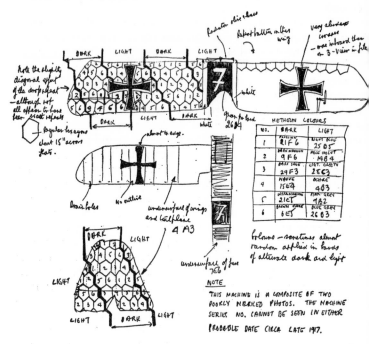

Austro–Hungarian hand-painted hexagons.

The above remarks apply of course to ex-works machines; repairs in the field would often have to be made with any odd length of fabric available, which would not necessarily be applied in the correct way or even be of the correct pattern. Movable flying surfaces – ailerons, elevators and rudders – and sometimes tailplanes did not always conform to standard practice. Because of their small areas and often irregular shapes, fabric might be applied to these components in whatever was the most convenient way, so that the pattern could run in any direction compared with that on the main airframe. Covering the fuselage was a relatively simple matter of making an 'envelope' of two, three or more longitudinal strips of fabric, depending on the size of the aeroplane, sewn together and laced up along the centre-line underneath. Sometimes ply-covered sections of aircraft – e.g. Albatros fighter fuselages or Gotha bomber noses – would be wrapped transversely in lozenge fabric to provide a hasty camouflage effect.

An interesting variation on German fabric finishes is the 'streaky' effect produced on some aircraft *circa* 1917 and excellently illustrated in the plate depicting the Fokker Dr.I. These aircraft came at a time when Germany was making every effort to use only cellulose for shrink-dope purposes and was evolving schemes to use dyes and other paint forms for its camouflage and markings. (The greatest shortage, incidentally, was of good red-pigmented materials, and explains why the use of red at this time was such a mark of the 'ace'. Only pilots of particular eminence could command the priority for materials in such short supply.) Over the yellowish (i.e. unbleached) linen Fokker tried applying a dark olive varnish, very sparingly, which gave a 'brushed-out' effect. This was then coated with a dark linseed-oil varnish which had the effect of transforming the dark olive to a brownish shade of green and the yellowish fabric that showed through it to a more orange shade.

These notes, brief as they are, show a few of the traps that exist for the student of aircraft colour schemes, and how easy it can be to fall into some of them. They will only be eradicated by more research, and by a wider publication of the results of that research. Many enthusiasts, in all parts of the world, are carrying out this kind of work with the same dedication and diligence that characterises Ian Huntley's efforts in this field. Sometimes the results of their labours are fortunate enough to get into print, but in all too many cases they do not. Through the medium of Blandford colour series it is hoped that the results of research of this kind can be made available economically to a wide circle of aviation enthusiasts who, for whatever reason, have a need for accurate reference on this subject. As already emphasised, verbal descriptions are especially valuable if they are based on first-hand knowledge or observation and can be related to a comprehensive colour dictionary – such as the one already cited or a suitable alternative such as the U.S. Federal Standard publication F.S.595a.

No single writer, historian or artist can hope to be a 'one-man encyclopaedia' of such a vast subject, and constructive help, be it in the form of fabric or paint samples, colour illustrations, verbal description of individual or national finishes, or any other form, will be welcomed – either by Ian Huntley, care of The Royal Aeronautical Society, 4 Hamilton Place, London W1V 0BQ, or by the author, care of the publishers.

APPENDIX 2

By Ian D. Huntley, A.M.R.Ae.S.

THE basic colour in which the upper surfaces of most British aircraft on the Western Front were finished has been referred to repeatedly in the past as 'khaki green' or even 'dark green'. The latter description is inaccurate, and the former sufficiently imprecise to mislead. The actual specification differed in constituent details over the four war years, but the early form, introduced as a varnish from 1916 onward, was mixed in a ratio of approximately 17 parts yellow ochre to 1 part lamp black (carbon black), by weight of dry pigment. This was not such an unbalanced mixture as it sounds, since the yellow ochre weighed fairly heavily while the lamp black was extremely light in weight. When mixed together the only possible pigmentation result is a khaki-brown shade, as discussed in detail later. What has given rise to the 'green' part of earlier descriptions is that, for protective purposes, this dry mixture was intermixed with cellulose acetate, oil varnish or some other glossy liquid medium, producing an optical effect known as 'green shift' which gave the finished coat a tendency to look slightly greenish under certain light conditions. (All British finishes, except some of the late-war night colours, were highly glossy in their original state.) An ex-works aircraft could therefore show a tendency towards a greenish-brown shade – though still predominantly brown – but once the material had 'weathered' after the aircraft had been in service for a while the effective colour was a positive brown. Re-created paint samples and the inspection of actual fabric samples from contemporary aircraft bear this out.

In later years, as an aid to production at a time of materials shortage, the two original pigments were mixed in their original proportions and canned under the name 'Standard Khaki'. It was added straight from the can to the most readily available base medium, and its final coloration was accordingly dictated by the medium chosen; for example, mixing with an oil varnish would produce a greater degree of 'green shift' than mixing with cellulose acetate, and both shades could be observed on one airframe, the former finish applied to ply panels and the latter to upper-surface fabric. (An incidental point, often overlooked in describing or illustrating World War 1 colour schemes, is that often this dark finish was carried round and under the leading, and sometimes the trailing, edges of the flying surfaces for an inch or two, depending upon the size of the aeroplane, giving them an 'outlined' effect when seen from below.)

The British khaki finishes

A protective coating or covering for the flimsy, fabric-covered flying surfaces of early aeroplanes was essential for two basic reasons: to keep the fabric stretched tautly over the main structure, and to prevent it from rotting under all conditions of use and weather. After various unsuccessful earlier experiments, an Advisory Committee for Aeronautics was set up in Britain in 1909 which, in conjunction with the Army (later Royal) Aircraft Factory, made a significant contribution towards solving this problem by evolving a series of P.C. (Protective Covering) varnishes. The Protective Covering studies were part of a series of experiments, started in early 1914, to find an ideal pigmentation that could be applied over clear-doped aeroplane fabric to shield it from the rapid rotting caused by the injurious (ultra-violet) rays of the sun. Most successful of the original P.C. series was P.C.10, then described as a dark khaki varnish, which afforded not only protection from the sun in a temperate climate but also a degree of camouflage when seen from above.

Patent rights on the P.C. series were taken out, and they became the only materials approved by the British War Office for use on the fabric of aircraft built for the Royal Flying Corps. The Admiralty's Air Department, being at that time a separate and autonomous organisation, chose not to be bound by the conditions imposed by the War Office, and freely purchased proprietary materials, including dopes and varnishes, which did not – and could not – conform to the patented P.C. series, in either constituent materials or colour, until R.F.C. and R.N.A.S. materials were standardised in 1916, following the formation of the joint-service Air Board. Before 1916, therefore, there were *two* forms of this protective finish: P.C.10 for aircraft built for the War Office, and Proprietary Khaki for aircraft built for the Admiralty.

Because of their 'freelance' nature, the Proprietary Khakis naturally varied in both chemical composition and hue, but the re-creation of many of these was facilitated by reference to published Admiralty formulae in which actual pigment proportions were given. Hence, in recent research to re-establish the nature and coloration of P.C.10, it was possible first to reproduce and eliminate a series of varnishes which were *not* P.C.10. Having done this, it was then necessary to isolate the original P.C.10 non-shrinking cellulose top-coat varnish from other finishing materials which, although using the pigments of P.C.10, were of a different chemical composition. (It is important here to realise two things. First, that the designation P.C.10 applied to the dry pigment used to colour the protective medium, and not to the finishing medium itself: in different chemical forms it was a constituent in at least four different forms of dope or varnish, producing in each a correspondingly different colour value. Second, that different media and systems of application over the years also resulted in different colour values.) The early varnishes incorporating P.C.10 pigments were applied directly to the fabric in three or four coats, followed by two or more top coats of clear, non-shrinking varnish. At a later stage, P.C.10 was applied in varnish form as two finishing top coats over five coats of clear, shrinking dope. The final P.C.10 dopes, using darker pigments, in greater proportions and in a different medium, were applied in three or four coats directly to the fabric.

Any assessment of P.C.10 colour values must, therefore, have as its basis the nature and proportions of the pigments involved. These were specified as natural oxide of iron (yellow ochre), darkened by the addition of a little lamp black (see opening paragraph). Ochre occurs in nature in a range of colours from dull yellowish-brown to light reddish-brown, depending upon the nature of any impurities in the soil where it is found and upon the proportion of ferric oxide (Fe_2O_3) which it contains; the greater the Fe_2O_3 content, the purer it is and the nearer it lies to the reddish-brown end of its colour range. Initially, the early P.C.10 varnishes called for a minimum ochre content of 30% Fe_2O_3, the first pigmented dopes for not less than 40%, and the later dopes not less than 60%. Although less critical to the final colour, the

183

degree of purity of the carbon black pigment was also dictated by the P.C.10 specification.

Thus the early varnishes, having a low proportion of Fe_2O_3 in the pigment and being spread thinly on the fabric, resulted in a light olive-brown hue. The later dopes, with a higher percentage of pigment (which helped to save cellulose), appeared denser, more opaque, and of a more yellowish-brown colour. The introduction of P.C.10 pigments in linseed oil and long oil (copal type) varnishes, again in different proportions and strengths, produced further variations in final hue. It is the variety of application media – oils, varnishes, cellulose – which, with their optical effect of 'green shift' on a newly-finished aircraft, gave rise in the past to the oft-repeated 'dark green' or 'khaki-green' descriptions of aircraft finished in P.C.10 shades. At last, the exposure of this fallacy is becoming more widely recognised, although regrettably it is still perpetuated by some 'authorities' on the subject.

One other factor to emerge from the wartime use of these finishes was that a cellulose medium cannot be applied over an oil-based one (although the reverse was acceptable in an emergency). This necessitated a careful system of identifying various finishes by stencilling doping code letters on the finished surfaces, and the Air Board sought to standardise a single doping scheme for the fabric of all front-line aircraft, regardless of service. In the event, however, materials shortages and distribution and other problems prevented this ideal from being reached and, indeed, the doping code system became of increasing importance as more and more alternative doping and paint schemes came into being. The three main classes of doping/finishing schemes were as follows:

Class A

Using a clear, shrinking cellulose dope with a top coat of non-shrinking pigmented cellulose varnish. Introduced in April 1916 and remained in use throughout the remainder of the war. Consisted usually of five coats of clear dope and two of pigmented varnish (e.g. P.C.10, P.C.12, NIVO or black). When used initially in a Class A scheme, P.C.10 varnish could be applied also to metal and plywood components, and ex-works schemes usually called for such an application.

Class B

Using an opaque, shrinking cellulose dope with a top coat of clear, non-shrinking cellulose varnish. Introduced gradually during the latter part of 1917. A much-improved scheme, consisting usually of three coats of pigmented dope and two top coats of clear varnish, the latter acting as a waterproofing agent. Finish lasted longer than that of Class A and was quicker to apply, but used greater quantities of basic pigment. Introduction of Pigmented Oil Varnishes (P.O.V.) was necessary for painting metal and plywood components, saving valuable cellulose while giving an oil finish to match cellulosed fabric. Partially phased out in 1918 in favour of Class C.

Class C

Using a waterproof, opaque, shrinking cellulose dope only. Introduced from early 1918, this was a much superior scheme giving a much longer-lasting finish, often with the application of only three coats. Like Class B, it saved basic cellulose but required much more pigment, solvents and softeners.

There were, of course, variations from standard. Some engine cowlings were left unpainted; in 1917 some aircraft appeared with P.C.10 cellulose on fabric upper surfaces and P.O.V. Standard Khaki (the official name of the P.C.10 P.O.V.) on the plywood and metal surfaces. During the early part of 1918, as Class B and C finishes called for greater quantities of basic pigment materials, a shortage of P.C.10 pigments led to the use of a dark grey P.O.V., or other shades of grey, as an alternative to P.C.10; and some aircraft, by mid-1918, displayed a mixture of grey P.O.V. cowlings and plywood surfaces, with Class B finish on the wings only. No one scheme completely superseded another, which was why the 'finishing marks' on the fabric were so important.

Summary

The designation P.C.10 refers to the khaki-producing *pigment chemicals* used in early experiments. The actual range of colours resulting from the use of those pigments depended upon their purity, their proportions, and the base medium with which they were mixed. The original specification called for this to be a nitro-cellulose (non-shrinking) varnish, but later specifications introduced acetate/nitro-cellulose (shrinking) dopes, spirit/oil varnishes (P.O.V.) and other media incorporating P.C.10 pigments, and each medium affected slightly the resulting coloration. Gradual weathering of aircraft in service affected this further still. Despite these possible variations, the control exercised over paint finishes from April 1916 onward kept them all within a fairly well-defined avenue of colour, and the table below shows the approximate colour 'envelope' of Methuen reference numbers within which the great majority of shades can be said to fall. This table is based upon 48 original samples of fabric, and 32 reconstructed paint samples made from original specifications. The early-war Proprietary Khakis of Admiralty-sponsored aircraft were greener by comparison, and came generally within the Methuen range 3 F 8 to 4 F 8.

P.C. 10 covering range, from light khaki varnish to brownish P.O.V.

FABRIC STATE	A	B	C	D
	Lightest	Normal	Dark	Darkest
	Greenish-ochre	Greenish-brown	Brown-green	Almost all-brown
New*	3 E/F 7	4 F 7	4 F/G 7	4/5 F 6
Moderate wear	3 E/F 5	4 E/F 5	4 F/G 5	4/5 E/F 4
Well worn	3 E/F 4	4 E/F 4	4 F/G 4	4/5 F 2
Average	3 E/F 5/6	4 E/F 5/6	4 F/G 5/6	4/5 F 4/5

* Based on Air Board colour master.
Note. – E or G values lighten or darken only marginally.

INDEX

187